THE
STRENGTH
of
MERCY

THE
STRENGTH
of
MERCY

JAN BEAZELY

foreword by
KAY ARTHUR

WATERBROOK
PRESS

All God's Children International is honored to donate all proceeds from
The Strength of Mercy to help and to extend mercy to the orphaned children of
Romania and Bulgaria.

THE STRENGTH OF MERCY
Published by WaterBrook Press
12265 Oracle Blvd., Suite 200
Colorado Springs, Colorado 80921
A division of Random House, Inc.

ISBN 1-57856-194-9

Library of Congress Cataloging-in-Publication Data
Beazely, Jan.
     The strength of mercy / Jan Beazely. –1st ed.
          p. cm.
     Includes bibliographical references.
     ISBN 1-57856-194-9
     1. Intercountry adoption—Romania. 2. Intercountry adoption—
United States. 3. Adoption—Religious aspects—Christianity.
I. Title.
HV875.5.B43 1999
362.73'4—dc21   98-53168
                                                        CIP

Printed in the United States of America

2005

15   14   13   12   10   9   8

To
Dorie Van Stone

You are a living example of the true strength of God's mercy.

*God used your heart and life to point us to the
abandoned and forgotten around the world.*

Our journey began at your knee, and in the Father's heart.

Contents

A Spiritual Adventure

So many times we think of "extraordinary" when we think of God. We think that what He does and who He works with always has to be extra-ordinary. We forget He is the God of the ordinary, working quietly behind the scenes—interweaving, entwining our lives with the lives of others as we simply walk in obedience to Him. Then comes the day when our mouths drop open in awe as we see what God was doing behind the curtains of time. And we drop to our knees in utter amazement and humble gratitude to the Lord for using us to impact another person's life in a way we could not have conceived or executed.

So it was with Jan and me. It began years ago with a quilt she made and sent to me at Christmastime under the prompting of the Holy Spirit. This was a love gift from the Lord, and I was so touched by this person I hadn't even known existed that I called information and got Jan's telephone number. This was unusual for me because I don't like to talk on the telephone. Yet there I was on Christmas day, calling a couple in Oregon I didn't even know.

The quilt and the phone call began a friendship between Ron and Jan and Jack and me that has become only more precious over the years. Eventually Ron and Jan sent their independent, strong-willed daughter to our Teen Boot Camp at Precept Ministries. Heather came kicking, screaming, threatening—and left a changed young woman. As a teenager, she went into Romania, where our ministry had been working secretly for years despite the oppression of dictator Nicolae Ceausescu. Right after his demise, Heather simply went into Romania, walked into an orphanage, and said she was there to help!

Her compassionate act eventually led to a most astounding story of God's using ordinary people in ways they least expected.

As you'll learn from reading this book, in the following years God drew Jan and her family into a marvelous adventure that resulted in their starting an adoption agency in 1991 to bring needy orphans out of Romania and Bulgaria and place them in the arms of loving families here in America. Little did I realize I was going to be pulled into that tapestry being woven by God.

Years ago our middle son, Mark, and his wife, Leslie, felt that someday they were to adopt a little girl. How wonderful it was to cross paths unexpectedly with Jan Beazely in Bulgaria several months ago and learn amid laughter and tears that the papers had been signed for Alexandra to become an official member of our family. My precious new Romanian granddaughter came home to us December 8, 1998!

There is a God in heaven, precious one, and He is at work in our lives, even when we don't realize it. The story you are about to read is an incredible testimony of how God can guide and direct the surrendered hearts of those who long to follow their Lord.

Living life with Jesus is meant to be an exciting adventure for ordinary people. God's plan for you will not look like the one He had in mind for the Beazely family, but He has a special and unique plan for you that will thrill your heart if you follow Him.

There is something significant in this story for you! Come on a journey that will strengthen your faith, challenge you to know your God in deeper ways, and create in you a desire to live the life you were meant to live—to be faithful in the ordinary so that God can accomplish the extraordinary through you.

—Kay Arthur

In Remembrance of His Mercy and Strength

This story could never have come to pass as it did had it not been for the strong support and unconditional love lived out each day within our family. When we struggled, we struggled together. When we rejoiced, we rejoiced together. My husband, each of our children, their spouses, and now my grandchildren have all sacrificed and unselfishly embraced the vision God has birthed in our family. Each used his or her God-given talents to help as the Father's plan unfolded. Although I have penned these pages, we have all lived out this story together and continue to make this journey side by side. I would like to acknowledge each of them personally, for they have been God's incredible gift to me. I am honored to be walking with them on the path God has laid out before us.

To Ron. Without your constant encouragement and faith, this book would never have become a reality. We began our lives together never expecting that we would be called far beyond the safe borders we had built around our lives. Thank you for embracing God's plan and for saying yes to the Father on that October morning in 1990. Now we don't need to wonder what could have been. We have lived firsthand His plan! What God has done is awesome. Thank you for your love and for the gifts of understanding and grace you extend to our family. You carry hour by hour God's heart for innocent, orphaned children. You are a wonderful husband and father not only to our own family, but God has made you a father to the fatherless around the world.

To Heather. I have watched you passionately embrace all God has had for you to do, faithfully enduring disappointments and even despair. Yet you have always stood firm and walked confidently forward, bringing "His sons and daughters from afar" to their new homes and into their new families. It has been my great joy to watch you walk in complete obedience to the Father. Your willingness to abandon all for the sake of God's call and for the sake of the children is an inspiration to me on a daily basis. Thank you for having the courage to go, the faith to endure, and the love to bring Hannah safely home. You are deeply loved.

To Hollen. Your faithful support and encouragement over the last years gave our family renewed strength and stability each day. Your personal sacrifices along the way enabled us to move deeper into God's call much faster than we believed was possible. God has marvelously gifted you in so many areas. As you now work side by side with your sister, it is wonderful to watch the Father blend your hearts to beat as one for the children. Your servant's heart toward all you meet and your willingness to go the extra mile on behalf of others are your own very special gifts. You are loved so much.

To Brian. Your caring heart and strong sense of justice have been gifts from God's own hand. You have taken to heart God's words, "Make justice the measuring line and righteousness the level." Thank you for working so diligently on behalf of the children. Your desire to walk humbly with your God and your willingness to touch lives as you relate to the older children living in orphanages are God-given abilities. I am proud of the man you have become, a man after God's own heart. Thank you for being such a wonderful son.

To Ryan. For the hours of care you have given Hannah over the years, allowing us to move at a moment's notice, a heartfelt thank-you. Your sensitive spirit continues to remind us of God's love and faithfulness. God has touched you with the needs of the world, and over the last years you have lived out His heart for those in need right where you live. Your willingness to embrace those in trouble is a wonderful gift from the Father. I love your heart, and I am so thankful you are my son.

To Hannah. You came to us wrapped as a little bundle of hope. You were an expression of God's grace and an example to all of His great mercy. Your presence in our family is a precious daily reminder of how much God loves us and how He moves mountains, topples governments, and performs miracles to bring us all home. The joy we watch you experience each day—just living life!—is an inspiration to us all. You are loved so very much.

To Calin. God sent you to Heather as an expression of His love and care for her. You have served as her protector, her encourager, and now as her husband. Your love for your country and the children of Romania is deeply imprinted on your heart. You have shared that deep love with our family. We have welcomed you as our son. Thank you for answering the call God issued first to your wife and then to you. You lovingly took her hand and with complete abandonment raced to embrace the destiny God had set before you.

To Doug. We couldn't have asked for a more wonderful husband for Hollen. You entered our family and became not only a son but also now a pastor and a wise counselor with deep insight into the struggles of others. Your support and encouragement to Hollen as well as to all of the family has been another of God's gifts to help us meet the challenges He has set before us. Our family wouldn't be complete without you and the compassion you bring to all whom God has called you to help.

My deep thanks to Jack and Kay Arthur. God has indeed bonded our hearts and lives beyond what we could ever have imagined. Thank you for your strong love and encouragement. From the very beginning, you cheered us along, supported us, and helped us immeasurably.

To Eileen Mason and Evelyn Wheeler. Thank you for believing this story was meant to be written and for beckoning this manuscript out of the depths of my heart. It was a privilege to work alongside you both. Your kindness gave me the courage to move forward.

To Liz Heaney. Your input was heaven-sent! I love your heart. God knew I would need you to get me through the process. Thank you so much.

My deepest thanks to the WaterBrook staff for hearing God and for working to make this book a reality.

Mercy's Legacy

Nothing touches me more than witnessing the "birth" of an adopted child into his or her new family. These tender transactions of the heart move even the most stoic bystander. They exemplify the power of a love that knows no borders or boundaries, a love that unites people across cultures and lands.

Adoption holds a special place in God's heart. After all, He sent His Son so that we could have the opportunity to be adopted into His family. Adoption is an act of mercy that originated as part of God's plan to bring us home, into His family. Adoption is God's idea!

The story of Moses is a wonderful example of God's adoption plan for a child. Moses was born to a devout Hebrew family at a time when Pharaoh was trying to kill all male Hebrew babies. His young mother, Jochebed, knew that she would have to find a way to protect Moses if he were to live.

The Bible doesn't explain why Jochebed decided to save her infant son by placing him in a basket among the reeds of the Nile. All we know is that Pharaoh's daughter found the baby crying in the bulrushes and decided to raise him as her son instead of turning him over to her father's guards to be killed. "When she opened [the basket], she saw the child, and behold, the boy was crying. And she had pity on him…and he became her son. And she named him Moses" (Exodus 2:6-10).

Who would have ever imagined this might be God's plan? Could it be God's will for Moses, a Hebrew, to be reared by Pharaoh's daughter, a pagan? Doesn't seem likely, does it? Yet God had placed Moses into this family.

One woman lovingly placed a small basket among the reeds; the other saw the basket and dared to open it. Both women were obedient. Both women were blessed. What a beautiful, awesome picture of God's sovereign ways and the place of adoption in His plan.

Down through the ages many birth mothers have made the same courageous choice. As I remember the beautiful portrayal of a mother's love in Exodus, I can't help but think of my own story. The same Father who orchestrated Moses' adoption also gave my husband and me our little daughter. And Hannah's adoption was the beginning of a grand adventure; it pointed our family toward other helpless and homeless children around the world who are waiting for new families.

This book is a testimony to God's faithfulness and to the strength of His mercy even for just one child. The world may view mercy as a sign of weakness, but God has taught me that it is an act of strength to extend mercy to those in need. Through His own marvelous mercy, God reaches down and stirs the depths of our souls. And even as He abundantly gives this incredible gift to us, we are all called to offer it to others on His behalf.

It is my prayer that our story will challenge you to answer your own family's individual call, that you will experience for yourself the incredible strength of His mercy. God is beckoning you and me to go beyond our safe places of comfort. May His mercy move your heart and take you further than you ever thought possible.

The LORD of hosts has sworn saying,
"Surely, just as I have intended
so it has happened,
and just as I have planned
so it will stand."

ISAIAH 14:24

CHAPTER ONE

A Promise and a Plan

With her little arms wrapped lovingly around my neck, four-year-old Hannah pulled herself close. Her head rested tenderly on my shoulder. Time seemed to stand still as I gently rocked her back and forth, savoring the sweetness of the moment. Then she abruptly interrupted the quiet. Her chubby fingers cupping my face, she insisted, "Look at me! Look at me in my eyes, Mommy."

I knew as I gazed into her deep blue eyes that something serious was on her mind, but I was unprepared for the heartfelt words that came tumbling out. "Mommy, how did you find me?" Her voice quivered. "How did you know where to find me in Romania?" The very thought of her lying in a little bed waiting for someone to "find her" brought tears to my eyes. Before I could answer, she continued, "Mommy, did you hear me crying? Did you hear me crying in my crib in Urziceni?"

Even at four years old Hannah had a vivid concept of the circumstances surrounding her birth. As I stroked her long dark hair, the words of King David flooded my soul. "Yet Thou art He who didst bring me forth from the womb; Thou didst make me trust when upon my mother's breasts" (Psalm 22:9). Oh, how those words comforted my heart. I had the assurance that the very hand of God had ushered Hannah from her mother's womb into our home. Her Heavenly Father had tenderly watched over her even as He began to move on her behalf.

As I cuddled my precious child, memories from the past four and a half years began to flow softly through my heart—memories that both humbled and thrilled me. Amazing experiences, both precious and painful, were already a part of Hannah's heritage. Miraculous moments…extraordinary events…sovereign circumstances—gifts to her from God's own hand. She had yet to realize the impact they would have on her life. Right now her serious four-year-old questions needed simple four-year-old answers.

"Mommy…Mommy…talk to me!" Hannah's insistent voice rang out. She was watching me intently now, waiting for my response.

So I began to tell my daughter her story—our story—a story from the very heart of God. "Yes, sweetheart, I did hear you crying. I heard you crying in my heart. No, we didn't know where to find you, but God did. You were never lost to Him! Your Heavenly Father showed Heather where you were. He knew before the world began that you would be born to be part of our family."

Smiling in simple faith, my little girl listened, taking in every word. Then just as quickly as this precious moment had begun, it was gone. Hannah jumped off my lap ready to move on, satisfied for now with the short answer to her questions. With a big hug, a kiss, and an "I love you, Mommy, sooo much!" she skipped away to play. I knew, however, that the time would come when she would want to know in detail the miraculous, extraordinary, and sovereign acts of God that had brought her from a country once held captive by a dictator to the shores of a nation where freedom rings loud and clear.

I tiptoed to the door of her room and watched Hannah happily share a tea party with our dog, Brie. She was oblivious to the emotions and memories that had surfaced within me as a result of her questions. Through Hannah the Lord turned the pages of my heart, reminding me that He had established a testimony—not only for Hannah, one child from one country, but a sovereign demonstration of the Father's tender love and care for all the little children of the world. I was reminded of the words of Deuteronomy 10:21: "He is your praise and He is your God, who has done these great and awesome things for you which your eyes have seen."

SILENT BEGINNINGS

When does God begin His special plan in a life? Is it when He gives a promise or when He finally brings the promise to pass? Although it may not always be obvious to us, there seems to be one distinct moment when God begins a new story in each of our lives. He writes words on our hearts that long to be spoken and strain to be lived out. Then with His own great hand, He begins to write the script. Experience by experience through seemingly ordinary days, He supernaturally orders our lives. Only when we look back and reflect on what appeared to have been the ordinary events of life does it become clear what a miracle the Lord has performed.

This is the story of a journey. Our family didn't write the story; we simply were given the privilege of living it out. As I look back, I am comforted by the assurance that nothing in our lives has been wasted. Every moment pointed us in an already-established direction. Our only real choice was to surrender our hearts and lives to God's plan. Our journey is one God set in motion for a very ordinary family, a family probably much like your own. We brought along a few strengths and many weaknesses, a little faith and great fears. Yet despite all our frailties, God led us day by day, one step at a time along a path that had been prepared for each of us before the foundation of the world. It was a journey that would eventually lead us to a calling to help the nations of the world.

It began on a typical October day in 1985. I had no indication that anything out of the ordinary would happen on this particular day. Then, into a seemingly common moment, God slipped an extra-ordinary word—a promise that would change the direction of the life of every person in our family.

As the day came to a close with the sun setting and shadows falling around me, I lay quietly on my living room floor, basking in the wonder of autumn. There's nothing like a fall day in Oregon. My younger son, Ryan, came over and rested his little head lovingly on my shoulder. We snuggled, watching the shadows deepen and the night descend. In this simple moment I heard God speak. Like someone with a delightful secret waiting to be shared, the Lord whispered this promise to my heart: "I'm going to give you another child."

My heart skipped a beat. "Was that really you, Lord?" I asked. Again the words flowed clearly and directly, as if He was making sure I wouldn't mistake them. "I'm going to give you another child."

The living room had grown dark. The moon cast a soft light across the floor, and Ryan now slept in my arms. I kept asking God how this could happen. I wanted further clarification about this revela-tion. Instead my only instructions were "Just trust Me."

I took the words God gave me and tucked them away in my heart. I wasn't sure what else to do with them. I know now that a seed had been planted, a vision had been conceived, but years would pass before I under-stood the significance of that lovely October evening. Now I know the evening was anything but *ordinary*. What happened was an *ordained* event, and God would use our oldest daughter to bring His promise to pass.

Carrying my little boy up to his bed that night, I thought, *Oh Lord, who's going to explain all this to Ron?*

GOD'S WAY VERSUS MY WAY

"Oh no, Mom's crying again!" It was almost a game our family played with me every time I would watch a program on TV that showed children in need. In a matter of moments I would be reduced to tears. Time and time again I would be overcome with grief over the suffering of children around the world. Occasionally I wondered if there was something more to my feelings. The hurt, the desire to do something was often very intense, but I would push the thought away and convince myself it was just the response of a mother's heart. I had no idea that what I discounted as ordinary compassion for hurting children was really something God would use in His plan for me.

The Word of God tells us that the Lord wants to give us the desires of our hearts in accordance with His will (Psalm 37:4). Sometimes we fear our desires and longings. We assume that our yearnings are not spiritual enough to merit God's approval. In reality, our deepest hopes often are rooted in dreams that God Himself has planted in our hearts. Without the pull of our emotions, that compelling sense that this is the direction we should go, I doubt we would ever have the courage to move forward.

At that point in my life, however, I had a lot to learn about the difference between God moving supernaturally to bring His will to pass and my own feeble attempts to fulfill His promises on my own. One Sunday shortly after God spoke His promise to my heart, a family in our church brought their recently adopted Korean baby to be dedicated before the congregation. Before I knew what was happening, those familiar emotions filled my heart. The longing to help— to rescue—a child overwhelmed me. As we left the church parking lot that day, I decided it was time to tell Ron about my desire to adopt a child. I planned to punctuate it, of course, with the fact that I believed God had told me we would have another child.

My revelation was met with a less-than-positive response, culminating in an emotional exchange as we pulled into our driveway. Our four children, who sat quietly in the backseat as we drove home, quickly retreated to the house. Once in the garage, surrounded by rakes, shovels, and hoses, my husband proceeded to tell me his bottom-line opinion of my news: "When you get your life together, Jan, then *maybe* we'll talk about this." Obviously he wasn't as convinced as I was that I'd heard from God.

Through tears I pushed, pleaded, and begged Ron to change his mind, to reconsider—all to no avail. He was armed with every reason known to man why God couldn't possibly be leading us in this direction. After telling me the emotional reasons why such a step would be a disaster, he started in on how much money it would take to bring a child from a foreign country and the challenging responsibilities we already had in rearing our four children.

Sometime Sunday afternoon two very exhausted people walked out of the garage. By then even *I* questioned whether I'd heard from God. My husband never let up, adamant that I work on my own problems before I took on the problems of the world.

THE PLEDGE AND THE PROCESS

What happens when our dreams don't seem to fit with the reality of our lives? What do we do when we feel that a promise God has given us will never come to pass?

A few days later, my hope shattered, I came face to face with what I had done. I realized I had tried to bring about what only the Spirit of God could accomplish. I had a promise, but God had the plan. I understand that the execution of God's plan did not depend on my husband's ability to see that plan. What mattered to God was my trust and obedience *right now* in the midst of the situation. When I finally accepted this—and it was not easy—I gently tucked God's promise back inside my heart.

As fall gave way to winter and then spring, God occasionally reminded me of His October promise. I still felt a stirring in my soul whenever I saw a hurting child, but I had ceased struggling. And with the surrender came peace. The Lord gave me the words of Jeremiah 29:10-11: "'I will...fulfill My good word to you.... For I know the plans that I have for you,' declares the LORD, 'plans for welfare and not for calamity to give you a future and a hope.'" God's good word to me had been the promise of another child, but it was just that—a promise. The fulfillment of that promise was in the future. As I accepted this, a sense of hope quietly settled on my heart.

A promise is a pledge of God's divine intentions for our lives.... His plan is the process He chooses to fulfill His promise.

Days and weeks became months and years. Sometimes when God asks us to wait, it's hard to remember that He really does have a plan. It may even be difficult to believe we heard God's voice in the first place, especially when there is no indication that His promise is *ever* going to come to pass.

The Bible is full of God's plans and promises. Plans for individuals, plans for nations, and plans for you and me as well. As I searched the Scriptures, I read time and time again about God's promises. There were big promises and little promises, but the most touching, faith-building promises for me were those given to parents regarding children.

Abraham and Sarah were promised an heir. Hannah was promised a son. God promised Moses' mother her baby boy would be spared from Pharaoh's sword, and Moses miraculously became the adopted son of the Pharaoh's daughter. Finally an angel promised Christ's birth. God revealed His plan and His promise to Mary in a very personal way, and she responded by saying, "Behold, the bondslave of the Lord; be it done to me according to your word" (Luke 1:38).

As time went on, I became more and more confident of God's ability to execute His plan for our family. I studied the examples of His promises to those who had walked with Him so long ago and realized that a promise is a *pledge* of God's divine intentions for our lives. I also came to understand in a deeper way that His plan is the *procedure* and *process* He chooses to fulfill His promise. We have the promise. He has the plan.

Today I can confidently say that God's plan has taken our family places we never dreamed of going! We have experienced the agony and the ecstasy of living, sometimes very dangerously, in the hand of God.

I've come to believe that God's promise is usually reasonably clear, but it's the plan—the outworking of the promise—that makes me stand at attention and takes my breath away. The plan is the blueprint, the roadway to the promise. We all walk an appointed way with events and circumstances often not of our choosing, but only He knows the way that we take.

Eventually the time came for God to reveal the next phase of His plan. One verse in the Bible would take on new meaning for me in the days just ahead: "He changeth the times and the seasons: he removeth kings, and setteth up kings" (Daniel 2:21, KJV). Never could I have fathomed that the removal of a self-proclaimed king—a dictator halfway around the world—would mark our family in such a profound and unbelievable way.

There is an appointed time for everything. And there is a time for every event under heaven.

ECCLESIASTES 3:1

CHAPTER TWO

The Triumph of Trust

Years have not stolen the memory of the moment I first held our eldest child in my arms. What I remember most was the promise I made to Heather that "birth" day, the words I whispered during the first hours and minutes of her life. Holding her gently against my breast, I promised I would do everything in my power to give her the most beautiful life possible. This tender moment is still deeply engraved on my heart.

A few months later my husband and I stood before the church as our pastor prayed, dedicating Heather to the Lord. I remember trying to understand what it meant to dedicate my child to the Father. Was dedication just a ritual that Ron and I were going through because it was the right thing to do in Christian circles? Or was it an act of obedience, a giving back to the Father what He had entrusted to our care?

That day I knew little of what the Lord would require of me. I could never have imagined that eighteen years later Ron and I would once again pray together on behalf of our firstborn. This time more than words would be required. We would hear the Lord say, "When you gave her to Me, did you really mean it? She's Mine. Let her go." All my hopes and prayers for my oldest daughter were not things I had the ability to fulfill. Only the Father could give my daughter the beautiful life I longed for her to have.

Trusting God with our children, especially as they get older, gives a whole new meaning to baby dedication. Over the years I have learned that no matter how much we pray for, train, or love our children, at some point each of them has to stand before the Lord on their own and be willing to follow wherever He calls.

FROM BABYHOOD TO BOOT CAMP

The memory of that dedication service faded over time, and sooner than we could possibly imagine the teen years descended upon our happy home. A private war began. My sweet baby daughter was on the brink of womanhood, and *rebellion* was the operative word. Ron and I felt we were constantly battling Heather. If we asked her to go left, she would purposely turn right. School, friends, and curfews became points of contention. As the war intensified, we appeared to be losing.

Somewhere in the middle of the turmoil, Ron and I realized we were not equipped for all that life was delivering. We began to wonder how we could possibly lead our children if we didn't have the answer ourselves. Over the next two or three years, both Ron and I began to see that hearing a sermon once a week was not God's idea of intimate communion with Him. We began to search for deeper answers.

In God's timing we were introduced to Precept Ministries, a Bible study ministry founded by Jack and Kay Arthur. It is devoted to teaching people how to discover the fullness of the Word of God in a personal way. As we began to systematically study God's Word, our lives started to evidence a strength and vitality we had never known. Like water being poured out on a dry desert, the Word seeped into our lives and dramatically transformed our outlook.

Naturally we hoped this development would filter down to our children. As our association with Precept Ministries broadened, we learned of a summer conference for teenagers held on the ministry's property in Chattanooga, Tennessee. In our enthusiasm Ron and I decided that we would send all our children to this program. Since Heather was the oldest, we informed her that she should plan on going to Tennessee the next summer for the two-week "boot camp."

Heather spent the next year fighting our decision. The weeks prior to her departure for camp were filled with threats and defiant statements that would have cut any parents to the very depths of their hearts. Ron and I argued and argued with Heather over our decision to force her into something she had no desire to do. As we drove to the Portland International Airport that June morning in 1986, our daughter sneered, "I may get on the plane in Portland, but after I get off to change planes in Atlanta, you'll never see me again." Fear raced like an electrical current through our souls. As she walked down the boarding ramp, I was concerned that she might not even stay on the plane until takeoff. I took the flight attendant aside and said, "No matter what she says, don't let her off the plane until she reaches Atlanta." Just to make sure, we waited until the doors were shut and the gate closed.

Ron and I walked solemnly back to the car, wondering if Heather would actually change planes in Atlanta and show up in Chattanooga. Would this trip be the beginning of another heartache? We were trusting God that we had made the right decision. It had been difficult, but we held firm.

A few hours later, I heard the phone ring in Heather's empty room. Her answering machine clicked on as I passed the open door: "Hi! This is Heather. Help! I've been sent to a prison camp in Tennessee. Please send food, letters, anything! I need your help to survive!" It would have been humorous, except for the fact that I knew she meant every word. The hours dragged by—ten hours to be exact—as we waited for some word that she had arrived safely. Finally the call came that our daughter had indeed reached her destination.

As the next two weeks unfolded, each day brought a small victory. From the very first phone call informing us that she was the only girl with a short, punk hairstyle and felt out of place among all the long-haired southern beauties, we saw God changing Heather's heart. On Father's Day, just a few days before the end of camp, we received another call. Our tearful daughter begged her father to let her remain at Precept for the rest of the summer. While it was not possible for her to stay, her request revealed a dramatic change in attitude.

When Heather reluctantly returned from Tennessee, we had no doubt that God had tenderly touched her life. The old ways and attitudes began to disappear. Heather made numerous trips to Tennessee during the next year for other boot camps and various conferences. The strong-willed child blossomed under Kay Arthur's teaching. It was evident God had a "call" on Heather's life, and I reflected in those early weeks on what such a call might mean for Heather.

I knew that my own life had been made up of many calls. I understand a call as a divine invitation to move in a certain direction. Its hows and whys can sometimes seem vague, however, as it is often just a preliminary glimpse into an ordained destiny. Second Timothy 1:9 reminds us that He calls us according to His own purpose and grace. God Himself issues the call, and He executes the plan. We're simply asked to acknowledge His call. I find acknowledgment the easiest part of the process. The true test comes in living obediently within the call. Many are called, but few submit to God's sovereignty when the result isn't what they were expecting.

"SIT DOWN; I NEED TO TALK"

By now, with a few years of parenting teens under our belts, Ron and I considered ourselves generally prepared for the normal confessions of teenagers. But we were caught off guard by the announcement that

Heather made to us one November evening in 1988. She was sixteen, a junior in high school.

"I want you both to sit down," she began. "I need to talk to you. Promise you won't say a word until I'm finished." Any parent knows before that conversation even begins that they're headed for trouble—a major revelation is about to take place.

As we sat together in our living room, Heather revealed her plan, something she believed was *God's* plan for her life. I remember hearing the words "Quit school…Get my GED…Work at Nordstrom's to get enough money to go to Bible school in Austria." The rest of her carefully prepared speech is still a blur. I felt the color drain from my face as she explained that she felt God had something for her to do in Europe.

Thank goodness my husband had a tighter grip on his emotions than I did. One of us needed to remain calm. He responded. I reacted. All I could think of at the moment was *Oh great! My oldest daughter wants to drop out of high school. Boy, have we blown it.* We spent the next many hours talking, arguing, crying, and then talking some more. Heather was convinced she was doing the right thing—obeying God, just like we'd taught her to do. We, of course, were not quite so convinced.

After hours of negotiating, Ron finally came up with a suggestion that seemed to make sense. Heather agreed to make an appointment with an administrator at the local high school, someone whom we knew to be a godly man. We told Heather that we were willing to abide by this man's advice—either direction—if she were willing to do the same. Knowing that school officials don't counsel kids to drop out of school, Ron felt fairly safe. We all agreed that it was a reasonable compromise.

The following afternoon Heather strolled confidently into Dr. Aryes's office. I'm not sure what the conversation entailed, but a couple of hours later we received an unbelievable phone call. "I hope you're sitting down," Dr. Aryes said to Ron, "because I have just advised your daughter to leave school."

"What do you mean, you told her to leave school?" Ron exclaimed. "Since when does an administrator counsel a sixteen-year-old girl to abandon her education?" Dr. Aryes went on to explain why he had given his blessing. He had never seen a student so determined, so directed, or so focused on what she wanted to do and where she wanted to go. "If you hold her back now, you may succeed in keeping her in school, but you'll risk killing her spirit and her God-given sense of destiny."

Heather promised to get her general equivalency diploma (GED) immediately. If she failed the examination, she'd stay in school until she passed the test. And so the adventure began. Meanwhile our relatives, friends, and neighbors had more than enough to gossip about. I really couldn't blame them. At that moment, we looked to the world like irresponsible parents letting our child manipulate us. But despite what everyone believed, we knew we'd made the right decision. We had chosen to trust God with Heather. She had seen us on more than one occasion buck the status quo. She had watched us walk paths that seemed out of the ordinary. As our daughter stood ready to spread her spiritual wings, how could we deny her our support? So our family stood together, silently bearing the whispers and stares of those who didn't understand.

The Bible is full of young people who heard God's call. It should have come as no surprise that God worked in the same way again. However, when God calls *your* child, it's not a Bible story anymore. It's a reality check. And it's your precious loved one, not someone else's.

What we didn't realize was that Heather's leaving school was a mere "baby step" of faith compared to what lay ahead. Thank goodness the Lord didn't reveal the plan all at once. Mercifully He led us one step at a time. When the second semester started in January of 1989, Heather did not return to high school. She had already earned her GED, and she had a full-time job at Nordstrom's department store.

AN UNCHARTED PATH

"Where's your father?" I asked the boys as I walked from room to room in our home. "I can't find him anywhere." In her basement bedroom, Heather's suitcase lay wide open on her bed. A school brochure was tossed close by. More than a year had passed since Heather's decision to leave high school, but her dream had not died. Her vision for Europe was still strong, and tomorrow my eighteen-year-old daughter would board a plane for Austria. She had worked hard, saved her money, and been accepted into Bible school. She would spend the spring semester in Austria at Taurnhauf and the fall semester at their school in England, called Capernwray.

As she prepared to leave, I was stressed out over all the last-minute details. Ron had been depressed for days over the thought of his daughter leaving home for the first time, and neither of us were thrilled by the knowledge that she would be traveling by herself to a foreign country. As I headed for the basement, still calling Ron's name, I heard Steve Green's song "The Mission" coming from Heather's room. When I opened her door, I found father and daughter sitting on the floor, listening to the music with tears streaming down their faces. The words of the song continued to ring out in the background as I heard Heather say, "I have to go, Dad. God's calling me to go."

The hardest part of loving your children is the "letting go." It's so easy to manipulate a child's decisions to satisfy our own needs and desires. We cripple our children when we deny them the freedom to choose to go where God calls, to pursue their destiny. As hard as it was to release Heather into God's sovereign hands, our peace grew as we believed we were being obedient. We wanted to allow God to be God in her life, knowing that our children were not born to glorify us but to glorify the Lord.

As we left that basement room, Heather handed Ron a special tape she had made for him of all her favorite music. "The Mission" was hand-printed on the front label along with a note:

> *Dad,*
> *Thank you so much for being such a wonderful father and friend. I will miss you lots. I love you very much.*
> *Heather*

The next day we gathered at the airport to say good-bye and send our daughter off.

A SURPRISING TWIST

"Mom…Mom…Can you hear me?"

I could hear Heather's voice, muted and muffled, coming from what felt like the other side of the world. Almost three months had passed since she first arrived at Bible school. Classes had been dismissed for the summer, and Heather had signed up for a mission trip with Operation Mobilization's *Love Europe* outreach. Now she was calling from a pay phone in Budapest, Hungary. The team from OM had been camping in a park just outside the city, ministering to the street children through skits and songs. It took hours to get a call through because of the long lines of people waiting for the only available phone in the area. I could hear kids laughing loudly as I strained to hear Heather's voice.

"Mom, I'm doing great. The outreach is over in two days, and I just wanted you and Dad to know I just bought a train ticket to Bucharest, Romania."

"You did what?" I thought I'd heard her wrong. "You can't do that!" I exclaimed. "Please, Heather, it's too dangerous. There are tanks still in the streets."

Ever the composed one, Ron grabbed the phone. "It's simple; you're not going," he said. "I won't allow it!" Heather proceeded to remind us that she had purchased the ticket with her own money and that she really didn't need our permission to go, but she did want our blessing.

"Where did this idea come from?" I asked her, trying to stay calm.

"I want to help the orphans, Mom. I know God is leading me to do this."

As I looked at Ron across the room, that familiar voice began to speak to my heart. *You can't teach your children to have a heart for the world and then say no when I call them to go into the world.*

It was as if God Himself had tossed a glass of cold water in our faces. Sometimes faith can be so uncomfortable! In a single moment God had asked us to jump to a new level of commitment and trust. We were being required once again to willingly surrender Heather into His care. This time we had to trust God with her in a country that had just fought a bitter revolution and was only now embracing freedom. It was a huge leap forward for all of us.

LESSONS IN TRUST

The Christian life does not always play out the way we expect: *I do this, God does that.* It's just not that simple. The choice to trust God isn't cushioned by deals and promises that everything will turn out the way we think it should. God's only promise is that He will work all things in our lives for our good and for His glory.

Naively we had believed we knew why Heather went to Europe. The Bible school experience in Austria had been a wonderful opportunity for our daughter, and it miraculously vindicated our decision to let Heather get her GED. But now the tests would be more intense, and we would be taken to deeper levels of faith than we had ever imagined.

The choice to trust God isn't cushioned by deals and promises that everything will turn out the way we think it should. God's only promise is that He will work all things in our lives for our good and for His glory.

As Ron and I surrendered, though, our faith grew. God continued to put us in circumstances that required ever-greater degrees of trust. Each time a new test came, we had to choose once again to submit to His plan. Ron and I clung to the conviction that, regardless of where she went, Heather was in the care and custody of the Spirit of God. To proceed with confidence we had to know the character of the God in whom we were putting our trust. We were learning that the true walk of faith is not for the fainthearted—or for those who like to call the plays.

Two years earlier our daughter had wanted to leave high school early. *Now* she wanted to go alone into a country that had just experienced a revolution, a country still trying to free itself from the grip of communism. We were committed to supporting our daughter as she struggled to hear God's voice and embrace His will for her life. There was no turning back. The truly great things God accomplishes through His people often are not achieved through major events but through small steps of obedience. We were about to see firsthand how God uses simple acts of faith to impact the world in a great way.

I will go before you and make
the rough places smooth;
I will shatter the doors of bronze,
and cut through their iron bars.
And I will give you the treasures of darkness,
and hidden wealth of secret places,
in order that you may know that it is I,
the LORD, the God of Israel,
who calls you by your name.

ISAIAH 45:2-3

CHAPTER THREE

For the Love of Freedom

Heather's love for the Romanian people was first nurtured by Dorie Van Stone, a missionary friend of our family's. As Heather was growing up, Dorie would visit us a couple of times a year, telling us of her travels into Romania to deliver Bible-study materials with Precept Ministries. Her accounts of Christians being imprisoned for their beliefs, of Communist repression, and of her encounters with the secret police made a lasting impression on all of us.

No one tells a story like Dorie. We all felt like we were right there with her, visiting the underground churches or smuggling Bibles and study materials into the hands of believers who were hungry for spiritual food. Through the years we had learned to love and to pray for this country that was under such great oppression.

When the Romanian revolution began in December of 1989, we received an excited phone call from Dorie. "Jan, Jan! Did you see the news? Did you see it? They are fighting in Timisoara. They are my friends, Jan, my dear, dear, friends. These are people I've told you about, the ones I've prayed with. I've been in their homes. Oh Jan, pray for Romania. Pray for freedom."

All of a sudden, distant events on the nightly news became very personal and close. Real people were fighting desperately for something my family and I took for granted: personal freedom.

A TORTURED PEOPLE

The Romanian people had lived for more than forty years under a communist regime. For the past twenty-four years they had been ruled by an exceptionally corrupt dictator, Nicolae Ceausescu. Driven by his lust for power, he saw Romania, a country of twenty-three million people, as his private possession.

Iron bars wrapped tightly around this struggling country. More than three million informants monitored mail and telephone conversations. Foreigners and citizens alike were spied on in every block and village, breeding an oppressive atmosphere of fear and distrust. The Secretariat, military leaders loyal only to Ceausescu, ruthlessly carried out his policies of terror.

Bucharest, once a beautiful ancient city, saw many of its residences and churches ravaged and destroyed. Medical treatment for the elderly was declared illegal. Birth control was forbidden, and every family was commanded to have at least five children. Parents were given monetary inducements to have large families. It didn't matter whether the parents had the means to care for these children; the state was determined to supply human resources for Ceausescu's ever-growing army, as well as laborers for government factories.

Religious freedom was nonexistent. Orthodox Church leaders often collaborated with Romania's Communist authorities. Churches had to register with the government and were subject to its approval. A friend told us of one occasion when Bibles legally shipped into Romania were confiscated and turned into toilet paper. Most Romanian believers gathered secretly in homes or worshiped individually in private.

Only God could encourage the hearts of His people as they nurtured their faith in secret places. Throughout these years of torment, the believers' only sanctuary was His presence, their only protection His power, and their only hope His deliverance.

Why did God wait so long to answer the prayers of His people? I do not know. I can only bow before a holy God, accepting His declaration in Deuteronomy 32:39:

> See now that I, I am He,
> And there is no god besides Me;
> It is I who put to death and give life.
> I have wounded, and it is I who heal;
> And there is no one who can deliver from My hand.

As Ceausescu continued to rule Romania, drunk with vanity and intoxicated with power, a sovereign God watched from heaven. He caught every tear, heard every cry. The pleas and petitions of His people moved the very hand of God.

IT STARTS WITH ONE

The Bible is full of incredible accounts of God delivering nations. He used Moses, Joshua, and David against the strongest and mightiest rulers of their day. Certainly Moses would not have set out in his own power to free the Israelites from Egypt. As a young man Joshua probably never dreamed he would be given the privilege of conquering the land of Canaan and watching the walls of Jericho fall. And how could David, leaning on his shepherd's staff, imagine that someday he would be a king of Israel? Yet God used each of these godly men to impact nations. They helped to set captives free, fought battles out of obedience, and remained faithful to what God had called them to do…no matter what the cost.

Even today God calls men and women to take a stand, to pay the price, to be willing to walk where He tells them to go. On that sunny December day in 1989, few people in Timisoara, Romania, could have had any idea what was about to take place. Although it is clear now that a coup was being planned, only God knew how to orchestrate events to bring about the rescue of the Romanian people.

The events leading toward the revolution had begun some months earlier with an unlikely man, a Hungarian pastor named Laszlo Toekes. Pastor Toekes had been trying to persuade his fellow pastors to take a stand against Ceausescu's systemization policy. Under this policy, villages and towns were being destroyed and the residents forced to move into high-rise apartment blocks, where they could be monitored and controlled. Toekes had been speaking out against the communist regime for years, and he had often endured persecution and intimidation. One day an eviction notice declared that he, along with his pregnant wife and son, would be forced from his home and placed under house arrest. For seven months, from April until December of 1989, the Toekes family and members of their parish fought to keep the Toekeses' home and his job as pastor. But their appeals failed. Finally the eviction was scheduled for Sunday, December 15.

Even today God calls men and women to take a stand, to pay the price, to be willing to walk where He tells them to go.

THEY CAME TO PRAY

One by one parishioners came to the church. Bent over with age, babushkas wrapped tightly around their heads, black shawls draped over their shoulders, the *bunicas* had come to pray for their beloved pastor and his wife, Mira. What else could they do? These elderly women could not fight the dreaded Secretariat with their hands. Instead they chose to fight in the Spirit, where they knew there was power. "I have been young, and now I am old; yet I have not seen the righteous forsaken" (Psalm 37:25).

They stood quietly, gathered in groups of two or three, their gnarled hands clasped tightly in prayer, believing. "For where two or three have gathered together in My name, there I am in their midst" (Matthew 18:20).

As the day dragged on, they were joined by Baptists, who were followed by Catholics. Then the Orthodox believers appeared and before long the Pentecostals. As night fell, a human chain of both believers and unbelievers, ethnic Romanians and ethnic Hungarians, stretched around the church. Shoulder to shoulder they stood, united by a common cause: the desire to protect their pastor and friend.

Finally the mayor appeared and tried to strike a bargain with Toekes, promising that he could retain his pastorate and home in exchange for his help in ordering the crowd to disperse. Toekes agreed and asked the people to return to their homes, thanking them for their love and support. But the crowd, sick of unkept promises and broken lives, refused to move. The mayor eventually left, hoping to discourage the crowd.

In the darkness and quiet of the moment, a railway engineer took out a bundle of thin, yellow candles, which he had hidden under his coat. He lit one, then lit another person's candle from his own. The flame was passed from person to person until each face was illuminated by the soft glow of candlelight. Then the crowd of several hundred people stood quietly singing and praying, keeping vigil throughout the night, refusing to move.

By the next afternoon the crowd had grown to several thousand. A few hours later someone dared to speak the words that no one had yet let escape his lips: "Down with Ceausescu! Down with dictator-ship! We want liberty!"[1]

In a moment's time, hearts once focused on their differences dis-covered the power of unity. It was as if God had spread a sense of destiny over the gathering in Timisoara. The spark of freedom had been ignited and now burned brightly in the breasts of young and old alike as they circled the little church. Faith pushed out fear as the cry was raised: "On to party headquarters!"[2] Thousands descended on the Communist Party building, destroying party banners and posters. Pictures of Ceausescu were ripped from walls and burned. The Communist emblem was slashed from the Romanian flag.

A revolution had begun.

THE COST OF FREEDOM

The crowd stood in rows before the party building, refusing to leave. Suddenly automatic weapons fired round after round into the crowd, and a row of children lay slain in the cobblestone square. The soldiers fired again, and three more rows of young and old alike fell to Secretariat forces. As one row of Romania's citizens fell, another stepped up to take its place.

Tanks rolled onto the streets and helicopters flew over the crowd as snipers fired from rooftop perches. The orders were clear: Kill the resisters. A young mother and her two children were mowed down by a tank in the city's Liberty Square. They died instantly. A group of citizens ran toward a cathedral, seeking protection. As they raced up the church steps, a round of bullets sprayed the entrance and all fell, their blood spilling down the stone steps.

The police taunted the crowd, killing without mercy, torturing those they captured. Still the Romanian people continued to stand, neighbor helping neighbor.

Some Eastern-bloc countries were liberated through velvet revolutions. For them freedom came softly, like a morning sunrise. For Romania freedom was to come in a blood-spattered revolution. The murdered rebels, some tortured beyond recognition, were dumped into unmarked mass graves.

Ceausescu was in Iran on a state visit when the uprising occurred. Upon returning he sought to blame the rebellion on the Hungarian minority. He scheduled a propaganda rally in Bucharest at noon on December 20 for the purpose of forcing the newly arrested Toekes into signing a confession that he had led the revolt in Timisoara.

As Ceausescu stood on the balcony of the central committee headquarters overlooking Palace Square, he began shouting his lies in a televised speech. Suddenly a small voice shouted from the back of the crowd, "Timisoara! Timisoara!" The people, silenced so long, could no longer be quieted. They began to shout, "Down with Ceausescu!"[3]

Surprised and shaken, Ceausescu tried to gain control of the crowd, but to no avail. The color drained from his face as he brought the rally to an abrupt end. The man who had spent twenty-four years orchestrating every detail of his image had overplayed his hand. Those present that day say that a spirit of freedom permeated the air. People no longer cared what it cost; they wanted to rid themselves of this monster.

The momentum that had built in Timisoara now spilled over into Bucharest. Wearing yellow, blue, and red armbands—the colors of their national flag—Romania's sons and daughters picked up outdated automatic weapons, sticks, pipes—anything they could find —and fought for freedom and liberty. One eyewitness said, "Death was everywhere. Secretariat snipers were systematically murdering students. It was very dangerous, but there was no fear in their eyes."[4] For the first time in years, they had the hope of freedom.

DEATH OF A DICTATOR

Shortly after his failed speech, Ceausescu and his wife locked themselves in the Communist Party headquarters. The demonstrations and fighting continued through the night. Just as the angry crowd began to enter the building, the Ceausescus escaped by helicopter, only to be arrested hours later in Târgoviste, a town north of Bucharest.

> "Can the prey be taken from the mighty man,
> Or the captives of a tyrant be rescued?"
> Surely, thus says the LORD,
> "Even the captives of the mighty man will be taken away,
> And the prey of the tyrant will be rescued;
> For I will contend with the one who contends with you,
> And I will save your sons." (Isaiah 49:24-25)

Have no doubt that God Himself contended with Nicolae Ceausescu and his wife, Elena. No human justice could come close to the penalty God would require of this man and woman.

On December 25—just ten days after the Romanian Christians had sparked the revolt in Timisoara—the mad dictator and his wife were tried quickly by a military tribunal, executed, and buried in unmarked graves. A jubilant country rejoiced and danced in the streets. One tearful peasant flashed a victory sign and shouted for all to hear, "I am old, but I am free!"[5] The terrifying siege was over.

The state television broadcast Christmas carols for the first time in more than four decades. Heat and electricity were restored. Food began to appear on store shelves. Pastor Toekes and his wife, taken into custody when the uprising broke out, were found safe. Their guards fled when they realized Ceausescu had fallen.

The courage of one man, along with the prayers and support of others, helped spark a revolution that God used to bring deliverance in response to the cries of His people. Whether the events that unfolded in Romania were a revolution or an attempted coup, as many now contend, God alone removes and establishes presidents and kings. "The LORD of Hosts has sworn saying, 'Surely, just as I have intended so it has happened, and just as I have planned so it will stand'" (Isaiah 14:24).

As Romania opened its borders, the outside world began to learn of the needy, forgotten orphans who were the tiniest victims of Ceausescu's brutal regime—literally, the "prey of the tyrant." Not only had God's hand been raised in deliverance toward the people of Romania, His heart had been extended toward the children. Across the world, relief organizations poured resources and manpower into helping the hurting men, women, and children of Romania.

A CHANGE IN PLANS

Now, just seven months later, we received Heather's phone call telling us that within forty-eight hours she would be traveling alone into this ravaged country. Before our phone conversation with our daughter ended, she agreed to call us one more time before she left for Bucharest. When she did, she had some sobering news. All seemed to be going as planned until she was standing in line at a McDonalds restaurant in Budapest. Suddenly a dark-haired man rudely bumped up against her. Turning around, she saw him disappear into the crowded restaurant. A few moments later Heather realized that her passport, visa, train ticket for Romania, credit card, and cash were gone. Frantically she searched the streets, looking for the thief, but she was unsuccessful.

Ron and I believed this could only be a sign from the Lord that she should either delay or cancel her travel plans. We tried to convince Heather to reconsider the trip, but she was still determined to go. She saw the intrusion as Satan's attempt to prevent her from following the Lord's call. She adamantly believed she was to go to Romania no matter what.

So despite our concern, Ron and I spent hours negotiating a new passport from the American embassy as well as obtaining a new credit card and cash from the American Express office. Meanwhile Heather set out to locate the Romanian embassy, where she could get another travel visa for Romania.

With her new passport in hand, Heather went to the embassy—only to discover that it was closed. Desperate to finalize her paperwork, she persuaded a guard to take her passport to an official. The guard returned sometime later with the new visa.

Heather's voice was jubilant when she called us with the news of the miraculous answer to prayer. Our doubts vanished as we heard how God had moved on her behalf.

Rather than again spending three hours waiting in line for a train ticket, Heather decided to fly to Bucharest. The whole episode was now behind her.

Heather intended to stay in Romania at least a couple of weeks, maybe longer. She had packed relief supplies and toys for the children. Jack and Kay Arthur were visiting a pastor in Brailia, and the plan was for Heather to see them before they returned to the United States. Her plans had been carefully made, and God encouraged her heart with this word: "I will instruct you and teach you in the way which you should go; I will counsel you with My eye upon you" (Psalm 32:8).

With God carefully watching and His promises tucked confidently in her heart, Heather left Hungary, bound for Romania.

Though He slay me,
I will hope in Him.

JOB 13:15

CHAPTER FOUR

Dream or Destiny?

Heather's plane touched down on Romanian soil around seven o'clock in the evening. Shells of old planes and burned-out tanks littered the runway, an ominous reminder of what had transpired just months earlier. As Heather made her way off the plane, she could see bullet holes in the concrete walls of the terminal. Stone-faced soldiers paced back and forth, automatic weapons slung casually over their shoulders.

Inside the terminal, Heather stood alone in a slowly moving line, waiting for her passport to be stamped. She had no friend to lean on, no American face to offer reassurance. Yet her mission to help the children and her resolve to make an impact on their lives grew stronger as she surveyed the scene. *How have these people lived under such oppression?* she wondered.

A stern-looking official checked her visa and stamped her passport. With a wave of his hand, he directed her outside and up some stairs to claim her baggage. Circling slowly around the baggage carousel lay her backpack and supply-filled duffel bags—ripped wide open. They had been slit from end-to-end. As she rummaged through the contents, she discovered nothing had been taken. Amazingly, even her red, battery-powered tape player was still tucked inside.

Heather grabbed her luggage and walked outside. She could see the empty guard towers in the distance. Even though there were no checkpoints, she felt as though someone was watching her every move.

Without warning she was surrounded by a swarm of taxi drivers, all trying to get her attention. Heather quickly picked out a friendly face and, juggling her backpack and duffels, headed for the driver's unmarked car.

There are a few things parents expect their children to remember as they emerge into adulthood, basic rules and principles that were first instilled in kindergarten. I can honestly say that on this trip my daughter forgot everything we had ever taught her regarding personal safety. Fortunately I didn't know about it until later. Safe and secure in our home some ten thousand miles away, I was having my own struggles trusting my daughter into the Father's care. I drew strength from the promise God had given me for Heather from Psalm 121:7-8: "The LORD will protect you from all evil; He will keep your soul. The LORD will guard your going out and your coming in from this time forth and forever." It was a promise that was to be fulfilled over and over again in the weeks to come.

We had made arrangements for her to stay in the town of Brailia with a pastor and his family. Her instructions were to stop in Bucharest overnight and call for someone to pick her up.

As the homemade taxi made its way into Bucharest, Heather requested that the driver take her to the Intercontinental Hotel. Our friend Dorie had advised her it "was the only safe place to be" in the city. The driver's immediate response to Heather's directions caught her off guard.

"Oh, you no want to go there," the driver said. "She is very expensive. You stay at my house instead. Free!"

At first she said no, but he persisted. Before she knew it, Heather had agreed to spend the night with a stranger and his wife. What had seemed like a fairly good idea soon turned into a frightening situation. The driver introduced himself as Eggar and went on to tell Heather that he had not been a faithful husband to his dear wife.

Even in the light of that information, Heather's decision seemed irreversible. By the time Heather realized that she had made a dangerous decision, it was too late to change the plan. If she acted scared it could force a confrontation with the man. If she asked to be let out of the cab, she had no way of knowing where she was or who might approach her—she might find herself in an even more perilous situation.

Heather spent that first night in Bucharest lying on a stranger's couch, unable to sleep for fear of being attacked, being eaten alive by mosquitoes, praying for the morning light to come. All she wanted to do was get to Brailia as quickly as she could.

The next morning Heather immediately called the pastor in Brailia, but Jack and Kay Arthur had already left, and there was no one who could come and pick her up at the moment. Desperate to get out of the taxi driver's house, Heather decided to skip her trip to Brailia, even though there was no way she could tell us of her plan.

THE FACES OF CHILDREN

Heather asked the taxi driver to take her to an orphanage in Bucharest. Eggar, anxious to please her as well as to make some additional money off this young American, drove down Kisself Avenue toward the Arch of the Triumph. Tucked back in a forest of trees sat an old yellow building, Orphanage Number One—one of the largest orphanages in Bucharest. After walking down the long pathway to the entrance, Heather rang the bell. The door opened, and she abruptly announced, "Hi! I'm Heather Beazely from Portland, Oregon, and I'm here to help you." Dr. Bojinca put her to work immediately.

Inside Heather found the orphanage overcrowded and lacking even the basic necessities. A very few toys had been donated by relief organizations or by parents who had adopted children from the facility. Heather's first job was playing with a group of two- and three-year-olds and taking them on their potty break.

The children sat stoically in a perfect row—a dozen three-year-olds perched on little potties. Waiting…waiting…and waiting some more, confined to their routine. It was Heather's job to keep them seated on their little pots for fifteen or twenty minutes.

Thankful that she had packed her small, red tape recorder and an Amy Grant cassette, she turned on the tape. As the music played, twelve sets of little eyes looked on in amazement and twelve sets of little ears strained to hear "Thy Word is a lamp unto my feet." Many had never heard music before. The words of that familiar Scripture set to music began to bathe the dark corners of the orphanage. As the words continued to flow, "…and a light unto my path…," they bounced off the high ceilings, warming the stark, empty room.

Heather began to sing along. Bending down, she spoke the words to each child as she touched them and kissed each little face. As she moved slowly down the row, tiny hands began to reach out, aching for her anticipated touch. When Heather was about three-quarters of the way down the row, a nurse burst into the room. Although she spoke in Romanian, she made it clear she wanted the music turned off. She curtly motioned Heather to hurry the children through their potty break. As Heather rushed to comply, the children who were waiting for their kiss and personal touch began to wail. Tears welled up in her eyes as she realized how much this small sign of affection meant to the children. Stepping back, she ignored the nurse and continued on, embracing the children until each one had been touched.

Oh, the power of a tender touch, the reaching out of a hand. The Lord knew how important it was. When He was on this earth, He let the little children climb onto His lap and hang on His arm.

Alone in the Darkness

Romania was struggling to rise from the ashes of communism, and the oppression that had engulfed the country through Ceausescu's long reign still hung in the air as Heather walked the streets of Bucharest. Students staged demonstrations in front of the government buildings, unhappy with the present administration. Distrust and fear were just beginning to loosen their hold on the hearts of the people. After a spiritual battle of enormous proportions, memorials to those lost still stood all over the city, and candles burned brightly both night and day in honor of all who had given their lives in the fight for liberty.

One afternoon as Heather looked for something that would remind her of home, she noticed that a Hollywood movie was playing across the street from her hotel. Happy to touch base with the United States even through a movie, Heather stepped into the theater. Leaving a couple of hours later, she noticed a gaunt-looking gypsy man dressed in old, brown polyester shirt and pants walking close behind her. He seemed to be following her every move. Not wanting to lead him back to her hotel, she veered toward the Presidential Palace.

As she crossed to the other side of the road, she noticed that he continued to follow close behind her. Although she walked increasingly faster, zigzagging from street to street, she couldn't seem to lose the skinny, hollow-cheeked stranger. Spying a small Orthodox church, Heather ducked inside, thinking he wouldn't dare follow her in there.

She lit a candle and sat to pray for perhaps fifteen minutes, asking the Lord to help. After a few more moments, Heather returned to the boulevard. Her stalker reappeared. Heather turned to go back across the street, frantically looking for someone to help her. Finally, she stopped at the small roadside cart of a peasant woman, handing her a few *lei* for a rolled-up picture. Distracted by her pursuer, Heather didn't notice what she was buying. She was frantic for a plan.

Glancing back she saw the man in the shadows, still watching her every move. A throbbing fear descended on her. Although people were walking by, she didn't know how to ask for help, and no one noticed the fear on her face. Just then a taxi came shooting down the street. Jumping abruptly from the curb, Heather waved the driver down. "Lido! Hotel Lido!" she gasped. As the cab sped away, the man moved to the curb and watched the taxi disappear.

Hoping he hadn't tried to follow in another cab, Heather rushed quickly into the hotel and took the old steel-caged elevator up to her room. Slamming her door shut, heart racing, she fumbled with the old skeleton key. No matter how hard she tried, it wouldn't turn in the lock.

Panicked, she raced down to the front desk. "How come my door won't lock?" she demanded.

Two very laid-back attendants smiled widely, "Our locks don't work."

"What do you mean your locks don't work? What if someone tries to get inside?"

"Oh, you don't have to worry. We will protect you."

"How can you protect me when you're down here and I'm three floors up?"

"Oh, no worry; we protect you." Looking nervously at the front entrance, Heather ran back to the old, rickety elevator and pulled the heavy gate closed. The noisy elevator began to rise again to the third floor. Running for her room, she slammed the door shut and began to cry hysterically, "God, why am I here? It's worse than I could ever have imagined. I'm so scared. I don't even have a lock on my door!"

In tears, Heather began to pile chairs, a small table, and her duffel bags—anything movable—up against the door. Then, exhausted and spent, she lay on the bed sobbing. Next to her lay the rolled-up picture she had purchased from the old woman on the street. Reaching out for the crumpled print, she slowly unrolled it. She could hardly believe her eyes. It showed a young, blond-headed girl holding a small staff and walking oh so carefully on a very narrow log across a deep chasm. An angel stood at her side, tightly holding her hand. The angel gazed down at the child, but the little girl kept looking straight ahead, walking forward in confidence, without fear. "Behold, I am going to send an angel before you to guard you along the way, and to bring you into the place which I have prepared" (Exodus 23:20).

Sometimes in our weakest moments God is accomplishing the most. What appears to be a dead end contains the seeds of God's new beginnings.

As she held the picture, Heather's sobs subsided. At the bottom of the tattered print were written these words: "Today, our Lord, we dedicate our lives to you. You are our guardian." Fear began to retreat and faith once again caught hold, replacing the doubt that had invaded her heart. Exhausted, she fell fast asleep, confident that the same angel God had sent to protect her during the long day now stood silently guarding the unlocked door.

Sometimes in our weakest moments God is accomplishing the most. What appears to be a dead end contains the seeds of God's new beginnings.

A PHONE CALL AT LAST

Meanwhile, our own drama was being played out at home. Five days had passed with no word from Heather. We didn't know where she was or even if she was okay. We realized that getting a call through to us was virtually impossible, yet every time the phone rang my heart would skip a beat, hoping that somehow she had managed to find a way. That afternoon we received a call from a woman in California who had just arrived home with a child from Romania. Heather had asked her to call and let us know that she was all right.

Several days later the phone rang once again, and through the crackle and static of faraway lines, I faintly heard our daughter's sober voice. She had moved out of the Lido Hotel and was living with one of the nurses from Orphanage Number One. Using this woman's private phone, she had miraculously gotten a call through to us in the early morning hours.

Heather choked back tears as she assured me she was safe. But even though her body was safe, I realized her spirit was disillusioned and hurt. The weight of a country filled with so much need, combined with the realization that she was unequipped to meet that need, was just too much for Heather to bear. Discouraged and depressed, she fell into the emotional trap that has snared so many older and more experienced believers: Heather measured her success by how she felt and what she could see. Her feelings were captured in a short letter she wrote after she had been in Romania for just a few days.

Dear Mom and Dad,

I thought I was stronger than I am. I thought I could handle this. But I can't. Every time I walk into the orphanage, I get sick to my stomach. Despite everything, though, I wouldn't have given up the experience for anything. I just am down because I felt so called to Romania, and now I feel like I have disappointed God and myself because I don't have the stamina to stay the full time. I just can't. I cry here every day because I am so lonely, and everything around me is so sad and depressing. I know that God only asks us to be faithful, not successful. I was faithful in coming, so hopefully that is good. I can't help but feel like a failure for not wanting to stay. Pray for direction for me. I can't find any. The children of Romania will be forever in my mind and heart.

I love you,
Heather

Heather never mailed the letter, but she gave it to us when she returned home. If I had known and could have changed places with her, I would have done so gladly.

Years earlier, when Ron and I had stood side by side in front of the church, holding Heather safely in our arms and offering her to the Lord, I didn't see the tears she would cry alone in a far-off land. I didn't see her walking by herself down the bullet-scarred streets where a few months earlier the citizens had fought for the freedom she already possessed. I didn't realize that my child would be called upon to leave mother and father and home to carry a little bit of justice to children that only God knew intimately by name.

We believed this dream of helping children in a distant land was the result of the call Heather had nourished in her heart for so many years. Now it appeared the hopes Dorie Van Stone had so tenderly nurtured in the comfort of our home might be only a pipe dream, not a divine destiny.

Not long after she wrote that letter to us, Heather left Romania, vowing never to return. As she boarded the plane for Hungary, we waited for the call to assure us that she was safely in the west. At that moment, no one could have dreamed how God would deposit into Heather's life a renewed strength for the task ahead, how His own hand would quicken her heart, revive and realign her battered spirit.

Yet less than four months later, Heather would once again find herself in the country she thought she had left behind forever.

But for now it appeared that Heather had failed. She was plagued with feelings of failure and doubt. We tried to offer encouragement, reminding her that if she had even helped one child, she had made a difference in the world. Nevertheless she questioned her call to help the children, and she wondered if perhaps she had somehow missed a turn in the road.

While Heather was looking from her human perspective, however, God was viewing things from His. What He saw was a young woman committed to doing the two things important to Him: acting out of obedience and standing firm in faithfulness, no matter what the circumstances. God was looking at Heather's heart. In His eyes she was right where He wanted her, standing in the center of His will, poised for His next command.

Amid her feelings of failure and defeat, Heather still stood quietly before the Father. She continued to ask for His direction and His guidance. She knew she had traveled to Romania out of obedience. That would have to be enough for now.

And your ears will hear a word
behind you,
"This is the way, walk in it,"
whenever you turn to the right
or to the left.

CHAPTER FIVE

The Still, Small Voice

Heather was now safe in Budapest, and I began to relax for the first time in weeks. She had called us the moment the plane landed, her voice revealing her relief. Sitting with her feet propped up against the wall in the Budapest airport, she had again mourned her failure and inability to accomplish more in Bucharest. She felt she had let the children down by not being able to stay longer, to endure what they lived with every day.

Around midnight, the night before we were to drive to Seattle for our daughter's homecoming, I settled into a hot bubble bath, hoping for a few solitary moments to reflect and anticipate the joy of tomorrow. Ron and the children were fast asleep. I grabbed my Bible and began to thank the Lord for taking care of Heather. My heart was so relieved that this test of faith was finally over.

Then I again heard the voice of my Father, speaking clearly and distinctly in my heart. "I'm going to show you a child. She will be in the pictures Heather brings home. I want to get this child out of Romania. I am fulfilling My promise to you. You will know this child. She will stand out among all the other children." Stunned, I could hardly believe the words my heart had just heard. My mind drifted back to an evening in my living room so many years before, and I remembered God's precious promise.

For the next hour or so I immersed myself in the Word. God gave me verse after verse to confirm His heart for the child He promised to show me, Scriptures that revealed His heart for all the children held captive behind doors of bronze and gates of iron. As I finally went to bed, I decided that, like Mary, I should ponder these things in my heart. I held them there, afraid to share with anyone what I knew I had heard.

A JOYOUS HOMECOMING

The next morning the family piled into our old station wagon and headed for Seattle and the celebration. I still held in my heart the revelation I had received the night before. As we waited in the international terminal, the homecoming seemed like a dream. Five months had passed since we had seen our daughter. Ron broke into tears when she walked through the door, and Heather fell into his arms. Even the boys got a little misty-eyed at this glorious reunion.

As we talked late into the night, it became clear that during these past five months our firstborn had matured beyond her eighteen years. Her time in Austria, Hungary, and Romania had expanded her heart for the world and deepened her compassion for others. Her time in Orphanage Number One had left its mark on her both physically and emotionally. Heather grieved over what she had seen, over what these young children had to endure.

The next afternoon I encouraged her to get her film developed right away. I was so grateful for one-hour processing! I still hadn't said a word to anyone about the thoughts churning in my heart and mind. I wanted to be sure. When Heather and her best friend, Heidi, came home that evening with her pictures, I sat with them looking through photo after photo—Hungary, the school in Austria, and at last Romania.

I began to flip through the pictures she had taken at the Orphanage Number One. Suddenly my heart leapt at a photo of a little girl in a yellow print dress, pink leggings, and red sandals. I knew beyond a doubt that this child peering back at me with big brown eyes was the one whom God had marked. She appeared in almost every picture. As I looked closer, I saw that one of her little hands was missing some fingers. I remembered the Lord had said she would stand out. Here was a physical sign that seemed to confirm what God had spoken to my heart. When I asked, Heather told me the little girl was named Romona.

Knowing me as she did, Heather immediately sensed something was up. I tried to conceal my emotions, but she persisted until I broke down and told her the whole story. She stared in disbelief, shaking her head "What about Dad?" she said. "He'll never say yes."

THE COURAGE TO PRAY

A few days later, when I finally gathered the courage to share my heart with my husband, I found that Heather was right. But having learned my lesson years ago when Ron and I had first discussed the possibility of adoption, this time I closed my mouth and listened. I knew that if Ron's heart were to change, it would have to be God's doing and not mine. So I put Romona's picture on our refrigerator door and prayed.

Heather returned to England the first part of September for her second semester of Bible school, this time at Capernwray. Several weeks later Ron came into the kitchen one morning and glanced at Romona's picture on the refrigerator. "We are not going to adopt this child, Jan." His tone of voice indicated how strongly he felt about the issue.

I remember a sense of grief descending on my heart, and I began to cry. Ron continued his outburst, "I've always done everything God has ever asked me to do. But I draw the line at this. We have four children already, as well as restaurants, clothing stores, and a daycare. I don't need any more responsibilities."

Through my tears God gave me these words: "You are my husband. I will submit to your decision. But the sad thing is, if you are wrong—if God really does want us to do this—we will never know this side of eternity what *could* have been. To me there is nothing more devastating than to miss what God has, what He wants us to do. Ron, we cannot coast through the rest of our lives relying on our past obedience. I don't want to stand before the Lord someday and have regrets."

Without a word or show of emotion, he turned and left for work. Romona's picture stayed on the refrigerator door, and I continued to pray. God faithfully reminded me that He was in charge, that my husband's heart was His department and not mine.

"WILL YOU TRUST ME?"

The next weekend we were attending a Precept training seminar in Lynwood, Washington. I left a few days earlier than Ron, who was scheduled to come up Friday evening. By now, of course, all of my Precept friends knew about Romona and were praying for a miracle. Heather had her entire Bible school praying as well.

Late Friday afternoon I headed out to the Seattle airport to pick up Ron. As I traveled south on the freeway, I felt overwhelmed with the love I knew the Lord had for Romona. I knew I was feeling the Lord's desire for the child He had pointed out to me, His desire to give her a home and a family to call her own.

As soon as I arrived at the airport, I went to the gate where Ron's flight was scheduled to arrive, and I found a quiet corner. I wanted to write down everything that I felt God had been saying to my heart. I tried to record it just as I believe my Father had spoken it to me that evening:

My holy hand of protection hangs over this child. You have been chosen and called for such a time as this. Be persistent and do not be distracted by other people's opinions. Walk in faith believing that I have a plan. I will make a way where there is no way, a path where there is no path. Obedience is better than sacrifice. Will you dare to live dangerously? Will you trust Me completely to do only what will ultimately be the best for you and your family? I see the cries. I will take you a new direction, and many lives will be touched as a direct result of your obedience. Remember, as you have done it unto the least of these My brethren, you have done it unto Me.

It felt good to see these words in black and white. A few moments later my sweet husband would come bounding off the Jetway. I knew that before the evening was over, I would share with him what I felt the Lord had told me.

"WHY US?"

As we headed back toward Lynwood, Ron looked over at me and smiled. He was excited about the weekend. I'm sure the idea that I would broach the adoption subject again was the last thing on his mind. "What's new?" he asked with an unsuspecting grin.

In a split second, I knew this was the right time. After weeks and months of silence, the Lord said, "He asked. Tell him." So I did. Simply and with little emotion, I related what had happened as I drove to meet him just a few hours before. As we continued along the dark Seattle freeway, it was very quiet inside our car. Ron hardly said a word for the rest of the drive. He just kept shaking his head. Meanwhile God was reassuring me that He would have to be the one to confirm His words to my husband. I was to be still. I knew that if I did not obey the Lord and surrender to Ron's authority in this, I would be out of order, guilty of attempting to manipulate God's will.

The rest of the evening was filled with the comings and goings of the conference, visiting with friends, and listening to Kay Arthur's message. When we finally got back to the room, it was late. Exhausted, we both fell into bed and didn't even discuss the day's events.

We woke up early the next morning, planning to meet friends for breakfast. Ron was unusually quiet. Standing in front of the mirror applying the last of my makeup, I glanced over and noticed him sitting in the corner of the room. He was silently staring at the picture of Romona that I had taken from the refrigerator and tucked in my Bible.

Turning the photograph over and over in his hands, he seemed totally unaware that I was watching him. I turned back to the mirror, and in that moment I heard Ron start to sob. I looked over to see him slumped over in the chair, tears streaming down his face. My husband was pleading with God. I heard him say, "I can't fight this anymore. Why would You choose us? We blow it so often. I don't understand." As he sat in that chair, I witnessed my husband's personal dialogue with his God, a tearful transaction with the Father.

A few moments later I sat on Ron's lap, my arms wrapped around his neck, and we prayed together, thanking God for His faithfulness. We put all the details of the situation in God's hands and asked for guidance on behalf of Romona as we prayed a blessing on her future. As we left the room for breakfast, Ron tucked the picture inside his shirt pocket and reached for my hand. Looking at me he said, "We're going to try and get this child out of Romania."

A GOD-GIVEN ASSIGNMENT

Unremarkable, seemingly insignificant responses observed by God alone become interchanges where God proves the heart, refines the will, and prepares His people for their destiny. We were watching the

Almighty's plan unfold before us. The beauty of God's way is that He often chooses those who are most ordinary, unknown to the world, raising them up without an announcement. Even at the moment when it becomes clear something out of the ordinary is happening, someone who is chosen by God can react in disbelief. Like Moses at the burning bush, they may be unable to accept the fact that God is calling them to a particular assignment. In those moments of doubt and struggle, God holds them in spite of their efforts to escape.

I was learning a critical lesson: We do not go into ministry; God puts ministry into us. Many try to reverse this truth. They have coveted someone else's call or sought a ministry that was not given to them by God.

Unremarkable, seemingly insignificant responses observed by God alone become interchanges where God proves the heart, refines the will, and prepares His people for their destiny.

Just like Abraham, who tried to produce an heir before God's hand moved in supernatural blessing on Sarah's womb, most of us have tried at one time or another to manipulate God's will to make it fit our time frame, our desires, and our purposes. This manipulation can be so subtle that we may not realize what we've done until it is too late. Then we find our flesh has given birth to an Ishmael. In time the fruit of destruction is born, and our self-appointed ministry cannot endure the inevitable tests that come.

In just the opposite fashion, a true ministry is birthed out of obedience. God is not looking for celebrities; He is looking for servants. His eyes search for those who can be moved by a slight nudge, who are just as content to toil behind the scenes in anonymity as they are to stand before thousands. Visions that are built outside the will of God, goals that are products of our own ambition, plans that are platforms for our pride will come tumbling down at the first hint of trouble. In contrast a God-given ministry will be God-sustained through any circumstance.

*

SPIRITUAL CONCEPTION

On Saturday morning, October 13, 1990, in a hotel room in Lynwood, Washington, God the Father took two hearts and knit them together as one. From that moment a child began to grow in our hearts. Just as physical conception is necessary to bring a child into this world, so a conception has to take place in the heart if two people are going to bring a child into their lives through adoption. We didn't have a blood test to prove her existence. I couldn't hold a piece of paper in my hand to verify her reality by the latest ultrasound. But God's promise of a child was as real as any physical pregnancy. A daughter was conceived in our hearts just as surely as if she had been conceived in my own body.

When we arrived home from Seattle, Ron and I immediately called a family meeting. Sitting together in our den, we shared with our children what we believed God had said to us. We stressed that—even though we believed this was the direction our family was to proceed—we wouldn't go any further until we were all in agreement. Adding another child to a family affects everyone, so we wanted the entire family to be of one accord. A stunning confirmation was forthcoming: All of our children were in total agreement. Hollen couldn't wait to go buy Gap clothes for her new sister. Brian offered soccer games. Ryan volunteered to share the family dog.

We called Heather in England, and she was thrilled with the good news. "I'm so glad Dad changed his mind because I have already written a letter to Dr. Bojinca, asking her to save Romona for us. The whole school was praying. I knew it would work out."

When we ponder how God can change a heart, the challenge often appears difficult and complex. When the Holy Spirit descends on a life, however, it is amazing to see how quickly and supernaturally He can do a work.

That Sunday night as I lay in bed, I marveled at what God had done in two short days after such a long wait. In just forty-eight hours the Spirit had accomplished what my flesh could not have attained in years: God had conceived a child in our hearts. We could see no further than that. What we didn't realize at the time was that in actuality God had also begun to birth a vision.

*Behold, I have put before you an
open door which no one can shut.*

REVELATION 3:8

CHAPTER SIX

The Cost of Surrender

What started out as our simple desire to adopt Romona soon turned into a highly sophisticated crash course in immigration requirements and Romanian and United States law. I sorted through the maze of documents with the tenacity of a lawyer, and my growing ability to communicate intelligently with Washington, D.C., surprised even me. Phone calls abroad became a common occurrence. Before long I could even contact the U.S. Embassy in Romania without breaking into a cold sweat.

Prior to this time in my life, I'd had no international experience. Now, however, I was working under a divine directive, one that gave me the best credentials of all. Romona's tiny face peering out at me from the refrigerator door provided constant encouragement. A month into the document-processing procedures I had mastered another language—one that took me into a world of notaries, certifications, and state seals. Every procedure, every new term became a link to Romania—and to our child.

One day Ron and I decided to drive to the ocean. We just needed to get away. I remember thinking how our faith was like the sea—ebbing one instant, flowing the next. One minute we felt strong and directed. Then without notice our spirits would plunge into darkness, captured by our fear of the unknown.

Along the way we stopped at a small shop where, with some

tentativeness, I bought a small doll. This doll became an outward reminder that God was working behind the scenes on our behalf and on behalf of our little girl. In the meantime the Lord was beginning a new work in our oldest daughter.

OF SHEEP AND SURRENDER

Living in a magnificent old English castle, Heather felt that Capernwray seemed like heaven on earth compared to the stark realities she had left behind in Bucharest. Together with young people from all over the world, she settled into the academic routine. This peaceful setting, with sheep grazing on a nearby hillside, was an ideal retreat from the hard realities of Orphanage Number One.

Although our daughter had enthusiastically embraced our adoption plans and had even written a letter asking for Dr. Bojinca's assistance, she had no desire to return personally to Romania. The call lay dormant and cold. Her secret hope was that if she chose to forget it maybe God would too.

I understood my daughter perfectly. We all look for somewhere to hide in times of defeat—we seek a place where peace prevails and our problems fade, even if just for a moment. God, however, finds us every time. He seems to enjoy talking to us no matter where we are. He has a history of conversing with His servants in caves, on mountains, and even out on lush green hillsides where sheep silently look on. God once called David out of the hills of Judea to slay a giant. And now hundreds of years later He was calling again, this time to a young woman in the rolling hills of England.

God's questions to Heather did not fall on deaf ears: "Heather, why are you running from Me? From what I've set before you? Are you willing to go back? Will you let Me touch your heart with what is breaking Mine—the children?" The struggle that played out in the serenity of that English countryside finally ended one sunny afternoon with a tearful surrender and a silent prayer whispered in the deep recesses of my daughter's heart: "I'll go back."

No angels sang and no one applauded; only the sheep witnessed another of the oldest of all battles, the war between the flesh and the spirit. God's Spirit conquered Heather's desire to stay safe and secure. In its place He birthed a strength that is the by-product of sacrifice and struggle. Within her surrendered heart came peace and a sense of destiny. When our daughter called to share her decision, we all knew that she would return to Bucharest on our behalf to bring Romona home. Heather's obedience was her supernatural passport back to the land that had left such a deep wound in her soul. Her heart still heard the cries of the children.

REFINING THE CALL

As I closed my eyes late one November evening, I had no idea that in a few short hours our vision would again be tested and our faith painfully tried. Ron and I were startled awake at six the next morning by the sharp ringing of the telephone. Sleepily Ron reached for the receiver. As he listened intently, I knew by the look on his face that something was desperately wrong. In fact I was sure someone had died. Unable to contain himself, my husband was now sitting up in bed shaking his head in disbelief. He hung up the phone and jumped out of bed. "We've lost her!" he cried. "We've lost her!" The orphanage director, Dr. Bojinca, had written Heather with sad news. Romona had been adopted the day before Heather's letter arrived.

Ron walked over to the wall and began pounding it with his fist. "Why, God? Why? I would have done anything for this child." Tears streamed down his face as he wondered aloud whether God had played a cruel joke on us. My heart ached as the news sank in. I cried out silently, "O Lord, please help us. Please give us something. I know we heard Your voice." I sat in the middle of our bed, pleading with God for understanding.

There in our bedroom in the early hours of a new day, our hearts raw and wounded by grief, we bowed our heads together and surrendered our wills. Once again came the voice of the Father. Like the sun rising, pushing its first ray of light through the darkness, the words that flowed quietly through my heart brought peace and understanding: "I showed you one...to give you another. Trust Me. You don't have time to grieve over this. If you do, you'll miss the child I have for you. I promise in the end you will see and understand."

Our hearts throbbed. Our spirits were sore. But in the midst of it all, we knew God was calling us to trust in His guidance. Obedience was the issue. This knowledge, coupled with sheer determination, propelled us forward. We knew we could not measure our faith by our emotions but only by our submission and obedience.

I thought back on all that had transpired to bring us to this point. I rehearsed again and again the words I believed we had heard from God concerning Romona. I continually reminded myself that God had never promised that Romona would end up in our home, just that He wanted to give her a home. We had known all along that the outcome of our steps of faith were in our Father's hands. We took an emotional risk. Out of obedience we had embraced her as our own. We knew He had used her life to lead us this far.

How do you say good-bye to a child God used to call you to such a step of faith? Ron had struggled from the beginning with the thought that maybe he would be incapable of loving an adopted child as much as one of his birth children, but God used the loss of Romona to put that issue to rest once and for all. In retrospect I don't think Ron could have ever overcome his reservations about adoption without Romona's little face tugging at his heart. God used her to give us a sense of urgency so we would be ready and in just the right place when He unveiled the rest of His divine plan.

Now as I sat holding the doll I had bought in faith, I heard the Father speak once more: "I promise there will be no loose ends in this for you." I knew in my heart that sometime, somewhere, somehow God would allow our life path to cross Romona's. How or when, I certainly couldn't guess.

As that painful day unfolded, the Lord graciously encouraged us. A music tape arrived in the mail. The words were like a cool balm to our spirits: "God will make a way where there seems to be no way." That evening we watched a Christian movie called *China Cry*. As the movie ended, a phrase appeared on the screen: "The promise was fulfilled, one day at a time." We sat in the theater, tears streaming down our faces, as God gently strengthened our hearts with His presence.

As we lay down that night, we were able to say, "Thy will be done." The last several hours had been unbelievably difficult, yet God had spoken clearly to our hearts. There was no doubt that He had reminded us once again to trust Him, and we were confident He would fulfill His promise to us, one day at a time.

THE FEAR OF DECEPTION

Leaning against our kitchen counter several days later, I gazed out the window. Thoughts, emotions, and questions threaded their way through my tired mind. The stress of the last few weeks still weighed on my heart.

I found myself in the middle of inexplicable circumstances because I had relied on what I believed to be God's guidance in my life and that of my family. As I had often done in the past, I kept coming back to the same questions: *How do I know I've really heard God's voice?*

How do I know that I haven't manufactured my own explanation for an event or circumstance in my life?

My desire to avoid deception made me step cautiously as I shared the situation with those around me. The response generally fell into one of two categories: Some stood right beside us, cheering us along; others hung back in the shadows of our lives with judgmental attitudes. We knew the latter didn't believe a word we said. They were just waiting to be able to say, "I told you so. God just doesn't lead that way today."

Others' doubts and my own questions and fears finally challenged me to study how God has spoken to His people in the past. By the time I was finished with my study, I realized that hearing God's voice and being nudged in a particular direction by His Spirit was not that unusual. In fact, this kind of guidance is an intrinsic and normal part of the lives of God's people.

The stories of men and women in God's Word serve as a constant reminder that God has clearly communicated with His people right from the beginning of time. When God spoke to Moses face-to-face as a friend, Moses responded by saying, "Let me know Thy ways, that I may know Thee" (Exodus 33:13). In giving Moses instructions to lead His people out of Egypt, God spoke openly and clearly, not in riddles or in secret (Exodus 3). Later the children of Israel depended on the pillar of cloud and that of fire—supernatural signs of God's presence—to guide them (Exodus 13:21). The powerful hand of the Lord daily brought comfort, direction, and deliverance to His people.

My spirit became more and more persuaded that the journey still lay ahead of us. As Moses prepared to go before Pharaoh to plead for the children of Israel, so we prepared to rescue not a nation but a child. Recent events simply meant our call had become a little more complicated, not that it had been rescinded. Instead of sending our eighteen-year-old daughter to an orphanage she was familiar with to bring home a specific child she had met already, we were sending her to find an unidentified child living somewhere in Romania.

As the date for Heather's trip to Romania came closer, the reality of sending our daughter back to this struggling country set in. As a quiet struggle took place daily in each of our hearts, we clung tenaciously to God's Word and to His personal promises to our family. We had trusted Him with our daughter just a few months earlier, and we knew He was asking us to do it once again. Thankfully, her mission was more clearly defined as she prepared for this second trip, and we felt a renewed strength.

God mercifully gave us a sense of destiny as Heather prepared to search for her sister. We knew we had a promise, and it was clear God had a plan; we just didn't know the details. As a family we were counting on God to show us what to do, where to go, when to proceed. It was a blessing that God in His great mercy revealed the path to us one small step at a time. I'm afraid that if we had been able to see ahead we would not have had the faith to believe it all would come to pass.

The Holy Spirit pursued our hearts. Even in our weakest hour of doubt, when our confidence grew dim, He lovingly breathed on the smoldering embers of our faith—and we once again caught hold of the Father's hand. In these moments when we feared we had nothing left to lay on the altar, holy fire ignited our hearts, and the fervency of our call was rekindled. We knew that God was testing our willingness to trust Him, no matter the outcome.

THE PARADE OF QUESTIONS

The questions and unresolved issues still troubled our thoughts even though our faith was being strengthened. Was I afraid to see Heather go back to Romania? Or was I really afraid of her going and failing?

Would "success" automatically mean we had heard God? Could failure mean we had heard Him just as clearly? I often questioned the Lord in the days leading up to Heather's trip. *Why Romania, Lord? There are so many people going and failing, unable to adopt a child. What makes me think we are going to be successful? So many have come back with empty arms.*

Even in our weakest hour of doubt, when our confidence grew dim, He lovingly breathed on the smoldering embers of our faith—and we once again caught hold of the Father's hand.

I was struggling to find release from the stifling grip of doubt. After a long silence I heard that still, small voice patiently and tenderly answer, "You will be successful in My eyes no matter what happens, as long as you're obedient—because I have told you to go." A sense of peace came over my heart, melting away the confusion and worry. In the end the only real question was whether we would surrender to what He asked. Was I willing to submit to God's plan, risking what I perceived to be our spiritual integrity, even if Heather came home with empty arms? My step of obedience was finally taken with no strings attached. I knew that God would take on the obligation to fulfill His promises to us; my part was to trust and obey.

As I turned to move on with my day, the Holy Spirit added a simple postscript: "You are to call this child Hannah." *Well,* I thought, *if He knows her name, then He certainly knows where she is.* I felt a strong sense of destiny, and I knew beyond a shadow of a doubt that it was God's will for us to find Hannah. Later I looked up the name Hannah and found it to mean "God's grace." It was indeed God's grace that would lead us to this chosen child.

And you will be called by a new name
Which the mouth of the LORD will designate.
You will also be a crown of beauty in the hand
      of the LORD,
And a royal diadem in the hand of your God.
It will no longer be said to you, "Forsaken,"
Nor to your land will it any longer be said,
      "Desolate";
But you will be called, "My delight is in her."
      (Isaiah 62:2-4)

At that moment I felt as if a mantle of grace had settled warmly and securely over our child-to-be, wherever she was. I sensed that no matter what her circumstances, God held her securely in the palm of His hand.

Do not be afraid....
Do not let your hands fall limp.
The LORD your God is in your midst,
a victorious warrior.

ZEPHANIAH 3:16-17

Blessed be the LORD, my rock,
who trains my hands for war,
and my fingers for battle;
my lovingkindness and my fortress,
my stronghold and my deliverer.

PSALM 144:1

CHAPTER SEVEN

Warfare of the Saints

As the time drew near for Heather to return to Romania, we could see God orchestrating every detail. It was like watching holy, invisible hands, moving in perfect rhythm. He moved a heart here and placed a person there. In exquisite unison everything was working together. Our sovereign God was putting the finishing touches on a plan that had been in His heart since before the foundation of the world. One step at a time, our family was being drawn closer to Hannah.

One morning toward the end of November, Heather called unexpectedly to say she felt God was leading her to travel to Romania earlier than the planned time, which was Christmas break. During the past few days I had also experienced a certain urgency to move up the travel date. As we prayed separately and talked together, we agreed she should leave on December 7. Her professors and the headmaster of the school were not too keen on the idea, but none of us could escape the growing sense that the time to move was now.

Reading the Bible that evening, I noticed that a word that kept appearing in the narrative of recorded events, the word *suddenly*. This word was becoming the intimate reality of my existence as we tried to keep in step with the Spirit. We found ourselves propelled at turbo speed into the very center of His will. It was an exciting yet scary place to be. One minute we were standing still, waiting. The next moment we moved at God's command, sometimes "suddenly." God had acted, giving us specific direction, and now we would see His promise come to pass.

> I declared the former things long ago
> And they went forth from My mouth, and I
> proclaimed them.
> *Suddenly* I acted, and they came to pass.
> (Isaiah 48:3, emphasis added)

One by one each missing piece fell into place. Through a friend we were miraculously able to obtain the name of a translator in Romania who would work with Heather as she searched for our little girl. Our documents were completed and approved in record time. Our "favorable determination" from U.S. immigration arrived the day before Heather was scheduled to travel. This letter would give our new daughter her visa to enter the United States. It was as if God had put a hedge around us, and I was reminded of Job. Not only could we see God working but we continually sensed His presence. Since that ominous test in October when we learned we had lost Romona, there had been only a few struggles—intermittent skirmishes with the Adversary that we had taken in stride. We were beginning to recognize and deal with the Enemy when he showed his face.

Then it seemed as if God removed His protective wall overnight, and we found ourselves in the center of a spiritual battle.

BATTLE ZONE

Heather's departure date was one week away when the restaurant we own was robbed in full view of a room full of customers. At eight o'clock in the evening, a man demanded at gunpoint that our teenage shift manager place all the cash register money in the man's bag. The thief fled in a waiting car. Minutes later one very frightened teenager called Ron at home. Police tried to comfort us by pointing out how lucky we were that no one had been shot. Robbers aggressive enough to perpetrate a crime with that many eyewitnesses usually don't hesitate to take desperate measures. We spent the next few days working with the police, dealing with the continuing fear felt by our employees, and evaluating our financial loss.

Our minds filled with questions. Had we done something wrong? Had we sinned? Were we going our own way? Were we out of God's will? As I prayed, God showed me that our position in Him had not changed. He had allowed Satan to make a move. He had allowed him to try and distract us from our calling. With God's permission, our Adversary aggressively began his all-out assault. He meant it, of course, for evil. God, however, intended it for good. "But He does according to His will in the host of heaven and among the inhabitants of the earth; and no one can ward off His hand or say to Him, 'What hast Thou done?'" (Daniel 4:35). God was allowing us to be tested. We were in a battle zone. We had believed for Hannah; now we must fight for her.

Two days later, just as we were clearing up matters about the robbery, a call came from our daughter Hollen, a freshman in high school, telling us she had been assaulted. The school police immediately apprehended the girl who had hit Hollen in the face. The assailant gave no reason for her unprovoked actions and was later found to be on drugs. Nevertheless, our time and attention were consumed by police interrogations, decisions on whether or not to press charges, and some intensive comforting of our daughter.

All of this stress was adding up just as we were making last-minute preparations for Heather's flight. On Thursday I finally was ready to take all my documents down to the bank to have them notarized.

Our paperwork had to be sent to Heather in England via Federal Express by 5:30 P.M., Friday, November 30. What transpired over the next twenty-four hours could only have been designed by Satan as a last-ditch effort to ensure my failure.

I had made all the necessary preparations for a final trip to Salem to finish the certification process. I had followed all formats and procedures to the letter. My plan was to get everything notarized on Thursday and make the hour's drive to the state capital the following day.

As I entered our bank on Thursday, November 29, for what I thought would be a quick notarization of my documents, I found myself face-to-face with a hostile bank employee. She decided she knew more about my documents than I did. She challenged their format and defiantly refused to notarize them. I remember glancing at the clock as it slowly approached five o'clock. I had to get the notarizations *now* in order to be able to drive to Salem the next day, or I would miss the FedEx deadline. As the hands of the clock went into slow motion, we squared off. My final words were these: "I will not leave this bank until you notarize all my documents. Call the Secretary of State's office in Salem to verify my format, and you will see that I'm correct." I sat down in a nearby chair as she angrily dialed the number. I was ready to cry.

In that moment the Lord spoke to my heart. "Jan, it's not her you're fighting. It's the Adversary, your unseen aggressor." I should have been ready for it, but I was caught off guard by how blatantly Satan had shown his colors. As the clerk slammed down the phone, I felt a renewed peace. Curtly grabbing my documents, she notarized every single one. My procedure had been correct. We had pushed through another obstacle.

The next morning I left the house eager to make the drive to Salem to complete the paperwork. It was raining, but I decided to make a brief stop at the nearby shopping mall. As I left and was pulling onto the mall perimeter road, I noticed an old white truck moving slowly down another lane toward the same road. As I started to drive on past, the truck accelerated. Out of the corner of my eye, I saw him moving toward me, and I accelerated, but I wasn't fast enough. The truck slammed into my little black Hyundai. My body jerked forward and then quickly snapped back.

Stunned and shaken, I couldn't move for a moment. There were no other cars in sight. As I got out and made my way toward the two men from the truck to exchange accident information, I didn't know that I was the victim of a staged accident, an insurance scheme perpetrated against women who drive alone in crowded shopping malls. Later I learned the men with whom I had innocently exchanged information that day were wanted in Oregon, Washington, and Montana.

As I drove on to Salem in my beat-up car, my spirit felt like it had also experienced an assault. I was battling something I couldn't see, but its manifestation in the physical realm was starting to take its toll. I was emotionally exhausted. My mind rolled back uncontrollably over all the circumstances of the past week, and I wept as I drove down I-5. My falling tears kept pace with the rain splashing against the windshield. "Lord, I can't go on," I cried out. "I'm so tired. This is just too hard."

Then the God of the universe began to encourage, touch, and soothe my soul. I felt His presence and I heard His voice: "I am going to give you a very needy, beautiful child. She will be a great joy to you and to your family." The tears flowed as He continued to speak: "In your weakness, I can be your strength. Let me carry you right now." I was immediately, supernaturally infused with a spirit of hope. It was a precious moment, one that continues to remind me of how God intimately touches our lives when our own resources are spent and we have nothing left emotionally to give. In the most unexpected places, He wondrously shows us His loving-kindness.

> Whom have I in heaven but Thee?
> And besides Thee, I desire nothing on earth.
> My flesh and my heart may fail,
> But God is the strength of my heart and my portion
>   forever." (Psalm 73:25-26)

Two hours later my documents were ready to go, and I began the trip back to Portland with them. As I left the parking lot, I noticed that the rain had stopped. The sun shone brilliantly through the diminishing clouds, and a rainbow arched majestically across the sky. It followed me all the way home! Just as God had sealed His promise to Noah, He was once again sealing His promise to us. "When the bow is in the cloud, then I will look upon it, to remember…" (Genesis 9:16).

LEARNING GODLY WARFARE

During this time of last-minute crises, the confrontation with Iraq had been heating up. As I drove home from Salem that day, I reflected on the valuable lessons on wars and battles that God had been teaching me through General Norman Schwarzkopf during Operation Desert Shield. At one of his interviews, he had shared that identifying the enemy was one of the first prerequisites of battle. Saddam Hussein was a visible enemy while our family was, of course, battling unseen forces, but the analogy still held.

Once the enemy was identified, the general's job was to develop a war plan. Whether he realized it or not, General Schwarzkopf's strategies came right out of Luke, Acts, and Philippians. "What you really must know," he shared, "is this: *When you are placed in command, take charge.*" He continued, "Once, you've established your authority, you need to remember: *Do what's right.*"[1] The clarity and precision of those instructions rang in my soul through those days of warfare that we faced. Jesus tells us in Luke 10:19, "Behold, I have given you authority…over all the power of the enemy." In other words, when Satan tries to defeat us, Jesus gives the believer the authority to "take charge." Schwarzkopf moved in confidence against Saddam because he knew it was his responsibility, he was confident, he had the weapons necessary to win, and he had spent time training and preparing.

We could move in confidence against the enemy of our soul because we had the sword of the Spirit and the full armor of God. God had given us the opportunity to train and prepare. We were ready when the time came to outline a war plan and to move in confidence. "Put on the full armor of God, that you may be able to stand firm against the schemes of the devil. For our struggle is not against flesh and blood, but against the rulers, against the powers, against the world forces of this darkness, against the spiritual forces of wickedness in the heavenly places" (Ephesians 6:11-12).

God's Word also has a lot to say about the general's second piece of advice: *Doing what is right*: "But in every nation the man who fears Him and does what is right, is welcome to Him" (Acts 10:35).

In our world today, the clear distinction between right and wrong has been merged into a gray blur. Even in the Christian community, the line often is moved to suit the circumstance. But God draws a clear line between what is righteous and what is unjust. Doing what is right is not necessarily just obeying the letter of the law. It also involves understanding and embracing the heart of God.

Philippians 4:8-9 speaks about God's expectation and standards: "Finally, brethren, whatever is true, whatever is honorable, whatever is right, whatever is pure, whatever is lovely, whatever is of good repute, if there is any excellence and if anything worthy of praise, let your mind dwell on these things. The things you have learned and received and heard and seen in me, practice these things; and the God of peace shall be with you."

In our world today, the clear distinction between right and wrong has been merged into a gray blur. Even in the Christian community, the line often is moved to suit the circumstance. But God draws a clear line between what is righteous and what is unjust.

After the war was won, General Schwarzkopf said, "There was one reason and only one reason we fought, and it wasn't for oil. It was because Saddam Hussein said, 'I'm going to rob and rape Kuwait and wipe it off the face of the earth.'"[2] We fought because what Saddam was trying to do was wrong.

In plain terms God is waging a war with Satan, who coveted the power and glory of God. The battle that resulted from that attempted "takeover" was won at the Cross, but the war will not be finished until Christ returns. God hasn't absolved us from the combat, but He equips us to fight through it.

By the time Heather landed on Romanian soil, we were dealing with the Enemy on a daily basis. We were not certain why he was so interested in one child from one country, but in the years to come we would realize that Hannah represented all the other children that God would lead us to. We could not see ahead, but God could. He was determined to teach us how to stand firm, to train us for battle. He was teaching us to put on our armor and to cast down the fiery darts of the enemy. Reading about spiritual warfare was one thing; it was quite another thing to engage in it.

I arrived at the Federal Express office back in Portland with only minutes to spare. Before sealing the box, I carefully tucked a delicate Battenburg lace envelope among the papers. It contained two precious items: a handwritten letter to a mother who lived on the other side of the world and a silver locket for her with a picture of my husband and myself inside. Although I didn't know her name, I knew our hearts would touch.

At last, the documents that would ultimately produce our new daughter's freedom were on their way to England. Halfway around the world, Heather was confidently waiting to receive the package. She was ready now to run the last lap in the race, the long distance home.

I will go before you and make the
rough places smooth;
I will shatter the doors of bronze,
and cut through their iron bars.

ISAIAH 45:2

Through Doors of Bronze and Bars of Iron

Through the gray morning mist of the English countryside, a shiny black cab wound its way slowly toward Capernwray Castle. For the driver it was an ordinary fare, a ride to the station to catch a train bound for London. He had no idea that he played a bit part in a sovereign drama. This production had been cast by the greatest director of all—God Almighty.

As the cab rolled to a stop in front of the beautiful English fortress, Heather appeared on the doorstep, backpack slung casually over her shoulder and arms weighed down by suitcases filled with relief supplies. When the news spread that Heather was leaving school before the semester ended, her classmates had alternated between support and behind-closed-doors gossip. Today as the cab driver began to pile piece after piece of luggage into the car, doors and windows were flung open and students gathered to say good-bye. Even though her decision seemed irrational to some, this step of faith was in fact at the very heart of the Capernwray mission: to live the life of faith, obedience, and courage.

I have no doubt that as light dawned on December 7, 1990, God watched carefully and lovingly as His child, our tender warrior, moved into place. Called for such a time as this, she was willing and ready to move at the Father's command. The days and weeks had revealed the magnitude of God's heart and His commitment toward an as-yet-unidentified orphan. And now this promise resonated within our hearts.

JUSTICE FOR THE NEEDY AND AFFLICTED

In Deuteronomy God declares His intention to provide justice for the orphan and show His love to the alien by giving food and clothing (10:18). He goes as far as to say that anyone who distorts justice for them is cursed (27:19). Throughout history, God has established and removed kings based on their ability to extend both justice and righteousness to the people: "Blessed be the LORD your God who delighted in you, setting you on His throne as king...therefore He made you king over them, to do justice and righteousness" (2 Chronicles 9:8). Righteousness and justice are the very foundation of His throne (Psalm 89:14).

The God of the universe continues today to be an advocate for the afflicted (Psalm 140:12). Whether in the United States, Romania, Bulgaria, or China, the call to action is the same: a cry for justice. Heather's call was to a child in Romania, to guard the paths of justice for one child. But all of us who name the name of Christ are instructed to guard the paths of justice right where we live. We are the ones who are to "establish justice in the gate" (Amos 5:15). Empowered by the Spirit, we are to strive to bring an end to suffering as we have opportunity.

Heather watched from the window of her cab as her friends at Capernwray slowly disappeared from her view, swallowed up by the rolling landscape. As the car sped toward the train station, both faith and fear rode with her. The peace and tranquillity of her stone fortress faded into the background, and haunting questions began their march through the corridors of her mind.

Did justice dwell in the wilderness of Romania? Even with a dictator now dead and gone, did righteousness remain? History has proved that in the very worst of times, God always has a remnant, a faithful few who endure, preserve, and stand against injustice. Even when "righteousness stands far away" and "truth has stumbled in the street" (Isaiah 59:14), they continue to believe and stand firm. Despite Ceausescu's efforts to stamp out all righteousness, God continued to remind us all of a critical truth: *Justice* is the measuring line and *righteousness* still stands as the level, even in a country where these words had only dared to be whispered in the past (Isaiah 28:17).

All of us who name the name of Christ are instructed to guard the paths of justice right where we live.... Empowered by the Spirit, we are to strive to bring an end to suffering as we have opportunity.

Heather had no illusions about what lay before her. She knew it might take months to accomplish her mission. The newspapers related story after story of hopeful couples traveling to Romania only to return home weeks, sometimes months, later—empty-handed. Although a Romanian family had agreed to let her live with them in Bucharest while she searched for Hannah, she could not help but remember how quickly trouble can lay waste to our most carefully laid plans.

Gone were the sunny days of summer she had enjoyed during her last visit to Romania; ahead lay the cold snows of December. Heat was still an intermittent luxury in this war-demolished country, and a hot shower was something to be celebrated. Gone also was our hope of Romona, the child already known, already waiting, and ready to come home. Instead Heather was commissioned to search for a child known only to the Father, in a country that was still reeling from a revolution, among a people desperately struggling to survive.

Heather's journey had begun—a journey toward justice. Her heart had been supernaturally stirred "to do His task, His unusual task, and to work His work, His extraordinary work" (Isaiah 28:21). Our family had no idea how unusual and extraordinary the coming days would be—not only for Heather, but for all of us.

MODERN-DAY SAMUEL

I watched the clock on our bedroom mantel move slowly toward the midnight hour. Ron lay beside me, sound asleep. With my heart I had been following my daughter's footsteps during the past few days. I knew that at that very moment she would be rushing toward Heathrow Airport. We had made plans for Heather to call us just prior to her departure for Romania, around 3:00 A.M. Oregon time. It would be our last contact with her for who knew how long.

As I lay in the dark, my mind retraced the path of God's provision over the last few months. Every day His leading and encouragement had been undeniable sources of comfort as we set our hearts to follow Him. I thought back over Heather's first trip, when my concern had been for her life alone. Now my concern was for another life as well.

As I waited for her call, I knew that this trip carried with it a mantle of mercy. It was a journey of hope, a journey taken by one of my children to give a life to another. One daughter was birthed into this world from my body. The other had been birthed into our family and hearts by the Heavenly Father. Both had been destined by God to be part of our family.

Who would have ever guessed or dared to dream that our once rebellious teenager would now be preparing to search for a baby, a chosen child? Just as the Lord sent Samuel to find David, I knew that the same Lord was sending Heather to find Hannah. God encouraged me with the story of Samuel's search: "I will show you what you shall do; and you shall anoint for Me the one whom I designate to you" (1 Samuel 16:3). The next verse says, "So Samuel did what the LORD said." As I waited expectantly for Heather's last call, God reminded me that we had done what He had said.

There were those who still did not understand, who thought we were foolish to take on the responsibility of another child at a time in our lives when we should be worrying about IRAs, not diapers. Some doubted our sanity as we sent our eighteen-year-old daughter into Romania. It *was* unusual. Nevertheless I was confident that the promise God had made to me that October evening so long ago was about to come to pass.

Ron woke to the phone call at three in the morning. I had never slept. Quickly the children—Hollen, Brian, and Ryan—assembled on the extensions. In the quiet of that night just three weeks before Christmas, our family prayed for Heather. We asked the Father to protect her and lead her to the child destined for our home. Half an hour after we hung up, our daughter was on her way to Romania.

FROM CAPERNWRAY TO BUCHAREST

As the plane descended into the international airport at Otopeni, just outside Bucharest, darkness already had fallen. A fluffy blanket of white softened the look of a city still engaged in a struggle for a better life.

Heather searched the faces at the terminal, looking nervously for Mariana and Christi, her contacts arranged by Precept Ministries' Eastern European directors. When her search produced not one familiar face, Heather went in search of a taxi. Though she couldn't reach her hosts by phone, she did have their address. This time she picked the oldest, frailest driver she could find—a wonderful Romanian "Papa."

After winding its way through the narrow streets of Bucharest, the cab finally stopped in front of a row of small homes hidden behind worn iron gates. With the help of the taxi's headlights Heather located the faded address. Knocking on the door, she was greeted by a sweet Romanian *bunica,* or grandmother. Once they overcame the obstacle of language through smiles, hugs, and gestures, Heather found herself sitting in the family's living room—the living room that would become her bedroom for the next weeks, maybe months. A few minutes later Mariana and Christi returned, and our daughter was introduced to her new Romanian family.

The next morning Heather didn't waste any time making contact with our prearranged translator. It turned out he was too busy to help, but he promised to send someone else. A few days later Gabi and Serban showed up. To say they looked like characters out of an old Mafia movie would be a slight understatement. An "I love sex" sign dangled from the mirror of their little red Olcit car. From a mother's perspective these two men were unlikely candidates for Heather's support system. God had, however, sovereignly selected these men to drive my daughter hundreds of miles all over Romania. They would be her voice in hospitals, orphanages, and maternity wards. They would be her protection when she stopped to eat at roadside stands and in restaurants.

With the help of her new companions, Heather's search for the newest member of our family now began in earnest. She pursued every lead during the first few days. Three possibilities looked promising: a three-month-old baby just outside Bucharest, a set of twins near Ploiesti, and a month-old infant in Alexandria. Before the week was out, however, it became clear that none of these children were destined to be Hannah Elizabeth Marie Beazely. Each had stood before

Heather, like David's brothers before Samuel, but she heard the same words Samuel heard from the Father: "Neither has the LORD chosen this one" (1 Samuel 16:8). By the end of the fifth day, the same scene had been repeated over and over again. No children available. Child just adopted. Parents willing to negotiate a sale.

We had decided before Heather left that we would not pay money for a child. As families and intermediaries asked for money to release their children for adoption, Heather continued to turn down their offers. Finally Gabi and Serban took her aside and in broken English explained to Heather the "Romanian" facts of life: "You will never walk out of Romania with a child unless you are willing to give something in return—*never.*"

A heated discussion followed, but Heather remained adamant: "I will not pay a bribe for a child. I will find one righteous woman in all of Romania who will give me her child out of love. I am looking for a woman who wants only a family and a better life for her child."

Shaking their heads over the tenacity and naiveté of this young American, Gabi answered, "In Romania you will never find such a woman. Your God will have to perform a miracle." Serban reiterated their strong convictions, "You'll never walk out of Romania with a child, unless you're willing to pay a bribe."

Finally Heather put the issue to rest once and for all. "I'll stay for as long as it takes," she said. Little did Gabi and Serban know that God had His own special plans for these two translators. By the time Heather left their country, they would see life a little differently.

Another day came and went. Our tender warrior and her two guardians continued to search towns and villages. They drove from address to address all over Bucharest, checking out every lead, following up every possibility.

Heather had been in Romania five days when they pulled up in front of a tiny shack. A very unkempt Gypsy couple approached them with a tiny baby named Roxanne. Heather held her tenderly in her arms. As she gazed into the face of the little child, she knew full well our family could possibly hold the key to the child's future life and well-being. Was this the one? In the next instant Heather's heart broke. The parents demanded seven hundred dollars. This was not the child.

TIRED OF DEAD ENDS

On the morning of December 14, Serban and Gabi arrived early. They had expanded their search to the towns and villages outside Bucharest. For the next three hours, the trio drove from place to place. At every stop they were told either there were no children or the child had already been adopted.

The Romanian countryside was particularly beautiful that day as they headed to the town of Giurgiu. The air was cold and crisp. Haystacks dotted the fields. Village after village slipped by the windows. However, even the sight of Romanian children happily playing alongside the road didn't lift Heather's spirits. There had been too many disappointments and dead ends in the last seven days.

She had begun the week with a strong faith and high hopes. Now she found herself no longer scaling mountains but sitting alone in a valley. She began to pray: "Oh, Father, I'm so discouraged. Did I really hear Your voice? I'm so tired of dead ends. There have been so many closed doors. I have listened for Your voice. Have I failed to hear it?"

The backseat of a little red car was an unlikely place for God to meet my daughter, but in that moment of need God spoke to her tired heart with these simple words: "Look for a woman by the side of the road." Even in the midst of such confusion, Heather recognized the voice of her Shepherd. In her enthusiasm for what she believed the Lord had said, she boldly told Gabi and Serban to keep their eyes open for a woman beside the road. I can only imagine the nonverbal language that must have passed between those two men in that moment!

But the sense of urgency prompting Heather to watch the road became more and more intense. As the car wound its way toward Giurgiu, everyone's eyes were glued to the road ahead. But no woman appeared. They hit a dead end. In this village, too, no children were available.

Still hoping for a miracle, Heather could not bear to give up. Despite Serban's insistence that they head back to Bucharest, Heather persuaded them to visit one more orphanage, another thirty-minute drive away. They checked the hospital for available children. Again they were turned away. Overcome with disappointment, Heather agreed to return to Bucharest.

As they traveled the long, straight road back, the sun dropped lower and lower in the sky. Emotionally exhausted from the day's disappointing events, she threw her head back against the seat and closed her eyes. "Please, Lord, bring someone to me. I can't take much more." The hum of the engine was hypnotic. "It would be so wonderful just to slip off into sleep."

Suddenly Gabi swerved to the shoulder of the road and brought the car to an abrupt halt. There, standing silently by a long line of tall trees was a young woman. No one else was in sight. She was dressed in layers and layers of ordinary Romanian clothing, and a bright-colored babushka was tied tightly around her neck.

As Serban spoke to the woman, Heather drew upon what little Romanian she knew, straining to understand what was going on. In an unbelievable moment, the young woman pulled back her coat to reveal that she was "carrying a child." Serban began to translate her words: "I am pregnant almost nine months. I would like to give my baby up for adoption. My husband is a very bad man. He is making my life and my family's life very difficult."

The woman promised to call Serban when she was ready to deliver the baby. He could transport her to a hospital in Bucharest. Serban gave the woman his phone number. She peered in through the window at Heather and smiled knowingly. Her hands folded tightly in front of her, as if in prayer.

As the car moved back onto the road toward Bucharest, no one said a word. God was quietly at work in the hearts and minds of Gabi and Serban. As for Heather, she might as well have been Moses standing before the burning bush. God had indeed gotten her attention. With a renewed heart, she recognized that holy hands were orchestrating every detail of this assignment.

Wait for the LORD;
be strong, and let your heart take courage;
yes, wait for the LORD.

PSALM 27:14

Chapter Nine

Waiting God's Way

A crumpled map, rescued from an old *National Geographic,* was spread out on my bed. Searching the borders of Eastern Europe, I finally located Romania. My eyes traveled the length and width of a country that until a few years earlier I barely knew existed. I wondered in that moment how we would ever find the one little girl who belonged to us. I prayed, laying my hands over large cities and small towns— mere black dots on the map, but full of lives and souls known intimately to the Father. I covered the country with my prayers, interceding for a child who was still only a promise.

Days had passed since our early morning call from Heather before her departure for Romania. We had no details about the difficult road she was walking. All we could do was wait, hope, and pray. Our verse of encouragement in those days was taken from Isaiah 49:23: "Those who hopefully wait for Me will not be put to shame." Our daily prayer was that Heather would find the path God had prepared for her.

While we waited, I grew increasingly aware of the fact that *waiting* was probably my least favorite thing to do. *Speed* has always been my operative word. If anyone could come up with a way to do something faster, more expeditiously, it was I. Why do *slow* when you could do *fast?* This time, however, there was no shortcut. No easy way. No quick answer. In the silence, all we could do was wait.

THE FINAL ATTACK

Back in Bucharest late one night, overwhelming waves of emotion washed over Heather's soul. The stress and pressure of living with five other people—relative strangers—in tiny quarters had begun to take its toll on her. The difficulty of life in a foreign culture, coupled with the pressure of an unaccomplished mission, simply added to her growing disorientation. Mornings she woke from a fitful sleep on the living room couch to the sound of her hosts' young children practicing on the old piano in the hallway. Many nights she fell asleep listening to Christi, a well-known Romanian opera singer, rehearsing for his next performance. For someone raised with a respect for privacy and many of the typical American comforts, it was a daily lesson in patience and long-suffering.

Earlier that evening Heather had written in her diary in an effort to sort out her confusion and discouragement. Finally she prayed: "Please, Lord, give me strength, wisdom, and courage to press on against the odds. Lord, lead us. Guide us. Love us."

The image of the roadside woman continued to haunt her. Was it just a random event, or did it somehow play into God's sovereign plan? Two days had passed, and neither Gabi nor Serban had heard from the young woman. Had it been just a moment of encouragement from the Lord and nothing more? Should she try and pursue this woman? Should she continue to wait for the promised call, or should she move on in search of another child?

Finally Heather's frustration and loneliness consumed her. She rolled over and buried her head in her pillow to stifle the sound of her sobs. All the emotions of the past two weeks poured out in the darkness and quiet of the night.

"God, I know you could wrap this up anytime you wanted to! Where are You? Why don't You do something? Every day it just gets worse. How can I accomplish something I can't even see? I don't even know if this child exists. I don't know if I even heard You."

Like King David centuries before, Heather cried out before the Lord. She called out to her God: "Save me, O God, for the waters have threatened my life. I have sunk in deep mire, and there is no foothold; I have come into deep waters, and a flood overflows me. I am weary with my crying; my throat is parched; my eyes fail while I wait for my God" (Psalm 69:1-3). "Hear my cry, O God; give heed to my prayer. From the end of the earth I call to Thee, when my heart is faint" (Psalm 61:1-2).

Her heart clung desperately to the promise, but her feelings and human frailties came flooding out before the Father. That dark night of doubt and tears turned out to be the Enemy's last attack. Heather didn't know it at the time, but she was standing on the very edge of blessing.

Exhausted by the emotion and the late hour, she finally drifted off to sleep. Having had this honest conversation with the Lord, she was filled with a sense of peace. All was well between Father and child. He had listened and heard a daughter's cry. "God is in the midst of her, she will not be moved; God will help her when morning dawns" (Psalm 46:5).

INTERCEDING ON HER BEHALF

Heather finally got a call through to us on December 14, seven days after she had arrived in Bucharest. She updated us on the children she had turned down, the bribes, her dynamic duo (Gabi and Serban), and the woman by the side of the road. Up until that evening we had assumed that Heather would bring home a three- or four-year-old. The thought of a newborn sent us reeling. We were unprepared for that possibility. Thoughts rushed in about the toddler-size clothes we had sent over with Heather and how an eighteen-year-old girl would take care of a tiny infant in a country where formula was almost nonexistent.

After all of us took deep breaths, we calmed down. Then Heather went on to tell of her discouragement and the spiritual confusion she had experienced. Despite her fatigue and disappointment, however, she told us she had decided to leave the woman by the side of the road in God's hands and continue her search for Hannah. We hung on every word Heather said, not knowing when we'd hear from her again.

After the call ended, it hit me that Christmas was less than two weeks away. The thought of our daughter alone in a foreign country and in the midst of such trial was difficult. It would be the first time in eighteen years that our whole family would not be together for Christmas. I tried to convince myself it was just one holiday and we could celebrate it later, but my heart was heavy. I had hoped that maybe God would miraculously give us Hannah immediately and allow our daughters to fly home in time for Christmas, but it wasn't to be.

Ron and I understood Heather's seesaw emotions. We each had lived the moments of defeat and faithlessness that are the prelude to victory in the Lord. We knew that Heather had just been through that kind of moment. Together we poured out our hearts for our daughter. We cried to a Father who issues an open invitation to everyone to "draw near with confidence to the throne of grace, that [you] may receive mercy and may find grace to help in time of need" (Hebrews 4:16). We knew God is often closer in our valleys than on the mountaintop, and we prayed Heather would continue to seek His face.

THE UNDERSIDE OF BEAUTY

In those days of concern for Heather and what she was going through, God brought to my mind a wonderful illustration He had given me years before. It has to do with life and the true nature of His work in us.

I have always enjoyed needlepoint. I learned the craft from a mother who used to spend hours creating exquisite masterpieces. But my mother's real love was the most beautiful form of needlepoint, a much finer and more intricate version called *petit point*. As anyone who knows the art will tell you, it requires the precision of a surgeon and the patience of a saint. Bending carefully over her work with a special magnifying glass positioned at just the right angle, my mother would move the needle up and down over the brown, honeycombed canvas, precisely spreading the threads of color. Each stitch was the size of a pinhead. Each color was carefully selected.

Our family had been called to be a part of a beautiful picture—God's masterpiece, embroidered by His own hand from the foundations of the earth. Our lives represented just a part of the picture, one thread of ordained events that would impact another family thousands of miles away.

I remember watching my mother as she followed her pattern. I'd see her work hour after hour, laying down thousands upon thousands of tiny stitches. To my young eye it looked quite ordinary—certainly not something worthy of such time. My assessment in the end was this: boring. Why spend so much time on anything that takes so long to complete? I preferred the *faster*, more immediately rewarding version of needlework.

Over the years, however, I began to appreciate the difference in the results. Constructed with the small, special threads, Mother's creations looked as if they had been meticulously hand painted by a master. Her love also went into her work, and the results were personal, priceless gifts from her heart.

Through the artful ways of my mother and her beautiful petit point creations, God helped me to understand and comprehend His plan and His heart toward our family, toward all families around the world. Our family had been called to be a part of a beautiful picture—God's masterpiece, embroidered by His own hand from the foundations of the earth. Our lives represented just a part of the picture, one thread of ordained events that would impact another family thousands of miles away. The incredible pattern of His sovereign stitches had been worked through the canvas of our lives with great love and infinite patience. In those early months, we had no idea how our threads would be woven into His sovereign plan or joined with many threads from other families. Nor could we have imagined the beauty of the picture God had in mind.

Now as Heather continued her search, I knew that the Father was bending intently over the earth in the same way I had seen my mother bend over her work. His eyes focused on both Romania and America; His magnifying glass in hand, He was carefully joining the stitches. There would be no loose threads in this picture. It was destined to be a perfect representation of His great love for a struggling nation and for two families who were separated by borders and culture.

Day by day the picture began to unfold. God had an intricate plan for each of our lives, and we waited and responded with rapt attention and hopeful obedience as the Holy Spirit gently but firmly moved everyone into position. Over those days we wondered what the pattern would look like when it was completed. What would Hannah be like? How would Heather find her? Would she come from an orphanage or a hospital? What circumstances would surround her adoption?

Weeks before as I sat at our dining room table I had prayed, *Oh Lord, what do I say to a woman who has birthed her child only to place her in my arms?* That night words of love had filled my soul for a mother whose life would be forever intertwined with ours. Beautiful threads ready at last to be woven into the fabric of God's sovereign plan. The words began to flow:

Dear Birth Mother,

Thank you for giving us the privilege of adopting your child. Our family has loved and prayed for your country long before the world came over your borders. We have wept with you, and our hearts have been heavy for what you have had to endure. We want very much to adopt a child from your country. We have trusted God and prayed for Him to show us the child He wants to add to our family. He has chosen, we have chosen, your child. This child grew under your heart, but she has now grown in my heart. She will be nurtured, loved, and cared for abundantly. She will experience the love of brothers, sisters, parents, and friends. Thank you for allowing us to carry on for you where you are unable to go. We will raise Hannah to reflect her Romanian heritage and offer her the opportunities and freedom America can give.

With great love,
Jan Beazely

I had carefully tucked my letter away inside a Battenburg lace envelope. It was now in Heather's hands, ready to be given in love to a woman whose heart had been linked miraculously with mine. Recalling that night of peace, I once more breathed a prayer that God would bless and keep both mother and child, wherever they might be.

Instead of bronze I will bring gold,
and instead of iron I will bring silver.

ISAIAH 60:17

CHAPTER TEN

Threads of Gold and Stitches of Silver

Heather woke up on Monday, December 19, to freezing temperatures and snow-covered streets. Gabi should be on his way to pick her up by now. Serban had come down with a cold, so she and Gabi would be traveling alone toward the north. As she glanced out the window at the white flakes gathering in the tiny courtyard, she wondered if it was even worthwhile to go out in such bad weather.

Her thoughts were interrupted by a car horn, and grabbing her coat and gloves, she stepped gingerly out into the snow. Gabi was hunched over a crumpled map spread out on the steering wheel. Heather climbed into the waiting car, and they began studying their travel options for the day. Together they agreed to venture north out of Bucharest toward Slobozia, to an orphanage Gabi was familiar with.

Despite the weather it was a beautiful day. The heavy city traffic finally gave way to the wide-open roads of the countryside. Snowcapped haystacks dotted the fields along the way. Children pulled homemade sleds while farmers drove horse-drawn wagons along the same road. As the car moved north toward the mountains, tall, snow-laden birch trees draped softly over the road, forming a fairy-tale-like passage through the forest.

In Slobozia, Gabi and Heather found the little orphanage tucked away behind a tall iron gate at the end of a quiet dirt road. Dodging potholes, they finally stopped in front of an old, faded yellow building. Gabi offered to brave the elements to see if the director of the orphanage would invite them in. He trudged through the silent courtyard with a hopeful heart, but when a matron answered the door, she shook her head emphatically, indicating an obvious no. She pointed insistently in a direction away from the orphanage.

To Heather's surprise, when Gabi returned to the car, he told her the director had suggested they try the maternity hospital a few blocks away. Off they sped. Moments later they found themselves face-to-face with a very rude woman doctor who dismissed them harshly. "We have no children here. Get out." Gabi and Heather made a hasty retreat back out into the snow.

Discouraged by the rude behavior and rejection, Heather was almost ready to give up for the day when Gabi suggested they drive a short distance back to the little village of Urziceni. "It's on our way back to Bucharest," he said, "and I think there is a small maternity hospital there also." Forty-five minutes later Heather found herself standing in front of a sign that read "Spitalul Urziceni 1894." Outside the entrance a couple of dogs begged for food and Gypsy mothers huddled with their infants. Along with several ailing elderly people, they were waiting to see the doctor, forming a sad scene on this gray day.

Once inside, Gabi launched into his usual speech: "This young girl is from America. She is searching for a child for her parents. Would you have any children who have been left for adoption?" Heather could almost speak the words in Romanian herself. She even knew the answer in Romanian as well: *Nu!* Body language usually gave the answer before a word was ever spoken.

This time, however, the scene changed unexpectedly. The attractive, young doctor sitting in front of them introduced herself as Dr.

Vorica Stanciulescu. Instead of the expected "*Nu!*" she gave them a kind look and a softly spoken, "*Da*, I do have a young girl here with a baby." Dr. Stanciulescu asked that they return in a couple of hours, when she would let them know if they could speak with the mother.

A glimmer of hope rippled through Heather's tired heart. As they left the hospital for lunch, Gabi puffed nervously on one of his many cigarettes for the day. Heather wondered to herself who this mother was. What had brought her to Urziceni? What was her story? Could this possibly be the child God had promised?

A WOMAN WITH A VIBRANT HEART

Florinella was eighteen years old, the second child of a hardworking Romanian-Moldovan family. Like thousands of others, her family had struggled through the merciless reign of Ceausescu. They made their home five hours north of Bucharest in Tecuci, a town set up high on the Romanian-Moldovan border.

Florinella was a beautiful girl with a kind heart. She was full of life and yearned to experience the fullness of the independence the revolution had brought. The fall of the Ceausescu regime had brought an end to the strict curfews previously enforced under the watchful eyes of the local Secretariat. Eager to enjoy some of her newfound freedoms, she convinced her parents to allow her to visit her older, married sister, Dorina. Florinella ventured to the village of Urziceni, where Dorina and her husband owned a small house and were rearing their three children.

During her visit the new privileges of freedom fostered a romance between a young man from a prominent Urziceni family and this shy young woman from Tecuci. Like thousands of young people around the world, they thought their one encounter, their one moment of passion would go unnoticed. They told themselves that no one would be hurt or ever know. After all, Florinella was going back home the next week.

That April day in 1990 seemed like any other day, but it marked a time that would live in Florinella's memory forever. She knew what she had done was wrong, but back home in Tecuci her secret seemed safe enough. After all, she was eighteen—almost a grown woman. Within weeks, however, she realized her secret encounter could not be hidden after all—a child was growing in her womb. But the father had refused to marry her, and Florinella was left to face the future alone.

Under Ceausescu abortion had been outlawed in Romania, but one of the "freedoms" brought by the revolution was the right for a woman to decide whether she would carry a child or not. Florinella's Greek Orthodox background and her own personal convictions dictated that she would choose life for her child.

Her mother cried, feeling that the turn of events was somehow her fault. What could she have done differently with her daughter? Her sister felt guilty as well. Florinella had been visiting her when the relationship started. Dorina tried to support her sister as best she could from a distance. The women were, however, most concerned that Florinella's father would find out. They covenanted together to hide her condition from him. The knowledge that his daughter was pregnant out of wedlock would shame and dishonor him. They could not bear to tell him.

Months later, when Florinella started to outgrow her clothes, she was sent quietly to Urziceni to wait for her child to be born. Scared and alone, she knew that her baby was destined for the orphanage in Slobozia unless God performed a miracle.

Florinella grew more desperate as the time approached to deliver the child. She had done something wrong, so how could she expect God to help her? Just last Easter she had listened to the priests recite words of faith as she had walked in the streets of Urziceni, carefully holding a candle to represent the risen Christ. Now she was in this dilemma. As the baby moved within her body, her pleas for the safety and well-being of her child became prayers. She knew it would be impossible to keep her child. All she could do was cry out to a God she hoped would hear.

But Florinella did not know the strength of God's mercy. She had no idea that her pleas for the life of her child had touched the heart of God, that He had counted her tears and saved each one. Her Father had heard her prayer (Isaiah 38:5).

A CHILD IS BORN

On December 12, 1990, Florinella gave birth to a baby girl. Standing close by were an elderly doctor and a nurse. As the baby girl was placed gently into the waiting arms of her mother, someone else was present that day as well—the most loving Father of all. The One who promises to be a Father to the fatherless embraced them both.

The baby girl was wrapped "Romanian style" in soft strips of white cloth. Her little face peered out from under mounds of blankets. She was laid carefully in a very old iron bassinet in a special baby room under the watchful eyes of a kind Romanian nurse.

Florinella was moved into a large room with eight other mothers who had just given birth. As she looked around the room, she knew that most of these women were very happy, looking forward to taking their babies home after their week-long stay. Things would be painfully different for her and her daughter. Her child would not be going home. She would be on her way to an orphanage, and Florinella would not have the joy of cradling her, feeding her, and watching her grow.

As the days passed, Florinella hoped for some miracle for her child. Every time she held the tiny baby and looked at her sweet face, she cried for her little daughter. Florinella's body was healing, but her spirit slipped deeper and deeper into despair. Dr. Stanciulescu and Florinella's sister, Dorina, both tried to help. Even her mother managed to sneak down for the birth of the grandchild she would never know. But no one could find a way to boost the young mother's spirits.

The morning of Florinella's seventh day in the hospital, December 19, she arose anxious and depressed. Physically she was ready to leave, but she was in emotional anguish. She clung to her baby daughter and nursed her lovingly, relishing every precious moment. Little did she know that the Father had heard her prayers, and at that very moment His answer was speeding toward her.

Around noon Dr. Stanciulescu came quietly to her bedside and sat down. Softly, she said, "I had a young girl visit my office just a few minutes ago. I think you should consider talking to her." The baby's tiny hand was wrapped tightly around Florinella's finger. "Would you like to meet her? She's from America, and she wants to adopt a little girl for her parents." Their eyes met. A tear slipped silently down Florinella's cheek. Without a word she nodded her head. The doctor squeezed her hand and left for her office.

THE PRAYERS OF TWO FAMILIES

When Heather and Gabi returned to the hospital that afternoon, Dr. Stanciulescu met them with a warm smile. She led them out the back door of her office and across the yard to the maternity area of the hospital. Inside, they made their way down the dark corridors of the old building. At last, they came to a dingy little room with glass walls. The doctor asked them to take a seat.

Before Heather even had a chance to sit down, a nurse returned holding a little, white bundle. Heather gently pulled back the blanket to see two big blue eyes peering up at her. The nurse placed the baby in her arms. In that moment Heather wondered how Samuel must have felt when the boy David finally passed before him. Had he felt the same supernatural, overwhelming feeling of love she was feeling? Did he study David's features as she now studied the tiny face of this child? *She looks like my brother Ryan when he was a baby*, she thought. *What a beautiful baby!*

Before she could speak, Florinella was ushered into the room. Taking the child from Heather's arms, she sank down quietly on an old cot tucked up against a wall. A very scared young woman sat lovingly holding her tiny baby girl. Heather waited for Florinella to raise her bowed head and make eye contact, but she didn't. Heather could almost feel the quivering frame of this dear girl. She wore her pain on her face, and her eyes reflected the burden she carried in her heart.

Gabi began to translate as Heather told her story. Then Heather and Florinella flipped through the pages of the family photo album Heather had brought with her. Florinella's eyes welled with tears. *How does one choose a family?* She only knew the answer to that question as she saw the faces and sensed the love in this family. She knew this might be the answer to her prayers.

Finally, Dr. Stanciulescu turned to Heather. Through Gabi she began a conversation that would change many lives. He slowly translated the doctor's words: "Is this the child? Is this the child you're looking for?"

Heather felt for a moment like she was in a dream. It was as if God's arms were wrapped lovingly around the little glass room.

Gabi then began to translate Heather's response. She knew without a doubt that, yes, this was the child. For just a moment Florinella raised her head. Looking Heather straight in the eyes, she said, "I will give you my child because I love the kind look in your eyes."

Money was never mentioned. No bribe discussed. Gabi was speechless. Heather had found the righteous woman who loved her child and wished only to give her a good life with a family. Time stood still as Heather realized that God had finally led her to Hannah. His grace had answered the prayers of two families, not just one.

Before the encounter was over that day, Dorina was called and was asked to pronounce her blessing over Florinella's choice. Once she heard the details, Dorina agreed that the baby should go to the United States with Heather.

What an amazing day it had been! As Heather and Gabi rose to leave, Florinella sat with her baby in her arms and the photo album still clutched tightly in her hand. A great burden had been lifted from her heart. She knew now where her daughter would live. She held pictures of a waiting family in her hands. Her child would never see the doors of an orphanage.

On an April day in Romania, one young girl conceived a child. On an April day in America, another young girl heard the sovereign call of God and conceived a mission. Nine months later, the girls stood side by side, evidence of God's incredible handiwork.

Heather reached out to take Florinella's hand. As she squeezed the slender fingers, both women knew that they had been called from opposite ends of the earth to experience together a miraculous moment. Each had traveled a separate path, but both had been lovingly cared for and guided by their Heavenly Father to this moment of destiny.

The two eighteen-year-old women looked at the child chosen to be Hannah Elizabeth Marie Beazely. One gave Hannah life. The other would be there to watch her live it. One had determined her personality. The other would help to shape her heart.

On an April day in Romania, one young girl conceived a child. On an April day in America, another young girl heard the sovereign call of God and conceived a mission. Nine months later, the girls stood side by side, evidence of God's incredible handiwork. Embroidered together by the Father Himself, they completed a masterpiece. They were the threads of gold and stitches of silver that He had promised.

As Heather and Gabi walked out of the back door of the maternity hospital, the snow had stopped, the skies had cleared, and the sun cast a reverent glow over the fresh blanket of white. A deep sense of peace settled over Heather's heart as they drove back to Bucharest. She had found her sister. She would return the next day to sign documents and begin the legal process. She had experienced firsthand the power of God. She had felt His great love for both a mother and her innocent child. She had walked hand in hand with her Father.

The promise had indeed been fulfilled, one day at a time. As the sun began to set, the Romanian sky lit up with brilliant shades of orange and red. It was a day Heather would never forget.

> By awesome deeds Thou dost answer us in
> righteousness, O God of our salvation....
> They who dwell in the ends of the earth stand in awe
> of Thy signs;
> Thou dost make the dawn and the sunset shout for
> joy. (Psalm 65:5,8)

*Let us hold fast the confession of our
hope without wavering,
for He who promised is faithful.*

HEBREWS 10:23

CHAPTER ELEVEN

A Promise Fulfilled

With every victory the Father often sends a time of testing.

High on top of the Carpathian Mountains in northern Romania stands an iron cross. Raised many years ago as a memorial, it stood through the nation's darkest hours as a silent reminder of God's presence. Even though Ceausescu had ordered its illuminating light turned off, the cross was never removed. Holy hands supernaturally protected the symbol of Christ's victory over death, even as churches were destroyed and believers were imprisoned for their faith. The intricate circles of iron that made up the holy structure allowed the wind to sweep through it no matter how severe the storms. It is said that if one climbs the mountain and stands beneath the cross, a beautiful sound can be heard. As the wind blows gently through the sculpted edifice, a melodic song floats over the valley below. The cross marks a place of sacrifice in much the same way that the altar on top of Moriah marked the place of sacrifice for Abraham.

Little did we know that within a few short hours of hearing that Hannah had been found, God would call us to walk to another altar of obedience and sacrifice.

SUDDEN COMPLICATIONS

Returning to the orphanage in Urziceni the next day, Heather learned that the doctors suspected the baby had an internal deformity that would require multiple surgeries to repair. They suggested that Heather and Florinella take Hannah to a specialist in Bucharest to get a second opinion. The prognosis could be grim if this tiny infant was not treated as soon as possible.

The phone call bearing this news hit us hard. We were unprepared for the possibility that the child God chose for us might bring unknown and undiagnosed physical challenges with her. We had discussed special needs such as missing fingers, toes, and clubfeet—conditions that were clear and identifiable. This news was another step in faith for us. Heather told us that we had to make a decision in less than twenty-four hours about whether we wanted the baby. She shared what she knew about Hannah's condition, and we went to work educating ourselves about what would have to be done to help her.

In a matter of hours I learned that one of the foremost specialists on Hannah's condition was at the Oregon Health Sciences Hospital in Portland. I was able to get in touch with him immediately and quickly explained what I knew. What did he think? What was his prognosis for her future?

Yes, he told me, she would have to have surgery, but he couldn't tell us anything further until he examined her. Now Ron and I began to ask ourselves some very hard questions: Were we willing to take a child with special needs? Were we called to help only if we were presented with a healthy child? Were we willing to trust His choice? Did we believe that God and God alone would be able to choose the child who should enter our family? We felt like Abraham standing on Mount Moriah, considering that his only son—his heir—was to be sacrificed. He had to die to what he thought God had said. We knew God was calling us to die to our expectations, to submit to His will and His plans, even if in that moment we couldn't understand His ways.

When Heather called for our answer the next day, I asked her only one question. "Heather, are you sure this is the child?"

Her clear, confidant answer settled the issue forever. "Mother, I know that this is the child God showed me."

Ron and I answered together, "Then if this is the child God showed you, we will take her in whatever condition God has chosen."

A CHRISTMAS GIFT

It was now just two days before Christmas. The dirty, red Olcit sped towards Bucharest, passing wagons and bicycles along the way. Huddled in the backseat, Florinella nursed her tiny baby girl. Fear gripped her heart as she considered the questions surrounding Hannah's condition. How could this have happened? Maybe God was punishing her for her sin. If the baby were as sick as the doctors said, would Heather still be willing to take her? These questions and more pounded her soul like the relentless rain falling outside. Why had things turned out like this? The magnitude of her responsibility came crashing down on her. Would she be forced to leave her baby at an orphanage after all?

Heather watched Florinella, unaware of her fear. She marveled at how much this young mother loved her child. God had indeed answered Heather's prayer for a mother who loved her child, a mother who was giving her daughter a new life in America out of care and devotion, not for financial gain.

As all of them walked into the concrete medical building, Florinella hugged Hannah to her chest. When the pediatric specialist, Dr. Maximillion, arrived, he motioned for Florinella to unwrap the baby. With trembling hands she removed the layers of blankets and cloths that protected Hannah from the cold December snow. Gently the old doctor bent over the baby and began his careful check. Heather's heart was pounding. Florinella's dark brown eyes were blinking back tears. Before it was over, Dr. Maximillion had summoned three other doctors to the room. Together they huddled intently over the crying babe. Whispering quietly, they continued to confer.

Lives are changed by moments like these. Events sometimes fall second by second into our hearts. They come in what seems like an out-of-control free-fall, but in reality they are sovereign events orchestrated by the Lord of Hosts. These are the moments where hope and quiet acceptance meet. A private place in each of our lives where God acts and we stand poised to accept His will no matter what happens. While we pray for what we believe to be the best way, we stand in obedience, prepared to walk the path He has destined for us. As Ron and I slept that night, doctors half a world away spoke the words that would impact our lives forever.

Dr. Maximillion finally lifted his head. "There is nothing wrong with this child," he said, smiling broadly at the trembling mother. "This little girl is perfectly healthy."

Hearts leaped with joy. Smiles broke out on faces that a few moments earlier had been furrowed with concern. The long night brought joy in the morning as Heather called with the news. Our hearts were embraced by His presence as we thanked our Father for not requiring what we were prepared to offer.

Two young women who would be linked together for the rest of their lives stood gazing down at the child. Two prayers ascended toward heaven. One prayer offered in thanksgiving for a child found. The other a plea for strength to place this beautiful child into the arms of another. Both hearts deeply thankful that this little one, so treasured and loved, was healthy after all.

Heather and Florinella left the cluttered old office with the baby tightly wrapped against the cold wind. Their heads were held a little higher. Their hearts were a little lighter. The sun was setting once again in the Romanian sky. Heather had hoped that through some

During her first trip to Romania in August 1990, Heather worked at Orphanage Number One, which is one of the largest orphanages in Bucharest. Standing in front is Romona, the little girl God used to lead us to Hannah.

This is the photo of Romona that I placed on our refrigerator while I prayed God would change my husband's heart about adopting a child.

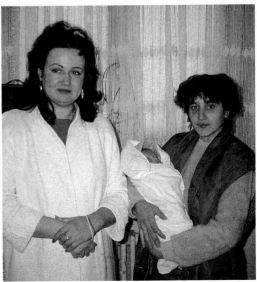

Dr. Vorica Stanciulescu, baby Hannah, and Florinella at the maternity hospital just days after Hannah's birth.

Florinella with Serban and Gabi, Heather's unlikely bodyguards. These two drove Heather all over Romania in their little red Olcit during her search for Hannah.

Heather rose to the daunting challenge of caring for an infant in a foreign country while she and Hannah waited in Bucharest for the final government approval of the adoption.

I greet my new baby girl for the first time as Heather places Hannah in my arms at the Portland International Airport.

What a joy to have a baby in our home once again! We had such fun decorating the nursery for the newest member of the Beazely family.

Hannah, four months old, gets a hug from Dorie Van Stone, the missionary who first nurtured Heather's love for Romania.

Six months after the adoption, Heather again met with Hannah's birth mother, Florinella. Heather was able to reassure the young woman that we are thrilled to have Hannah as part of our family.

I had the opportunity to meet Florinella in June 1991. How incredible to stand face to face with the woman who followed God's leading to give us a beautiful daughter!

Heather chats with a little girl during her visit to a Bulgarian orphanage in 1992.

Heather and the adoptive mothers of the first group of children brought out of Bulgaria through All God's Children International.

As you can see in this photo of Hannah at age four, Ron is thoroughly smitten with the daughter he once thought would never join our family.

miraculous circumstances she might be able to bring Hannah home to us by Christmas. It never hurts to hope, but God's sovereign plan had to be accepted. Much remained to be done—papers to file, a court date to attend, and an adoption decree to be notarized.

The late hour meant that the birth certificate could not be registered in the court that day, so Heather and Florinella had to return to the maternity hospital in Urziceni. Even though Heather longed to spend Christmas with her new little sister, it seemed right that Florinella should be able to spend one last day with her little girl. On Christmas Eve our oldest daughter walked the snowy streets of Bucharest singing Christmas carols with newfound friends. One young man held a Romanian flag, the wind blowing through the large hole where the communist symbol had been cut out. Just a year earlier these same streets were filled with cries of freedom. The happy group stopped in front of the United States ambassador's home, where they were greeted warmly. They all sang and celebrated together. A clock struck midnight. Christmas 1990 settled over the struggling country. One could hear the hope in the voices of the people.

TWO HEARTS UNITED

On December 26 Florinella laid the sleeping baby gently into Heather's outstretched arms. Together they visited the notary, and Florinella signed the papers giving her voluntary consent to Hannah's adoption. As painful as it was, Florinella knew that God had made a way for her and her child. His mercy had reached down and rescued her. Even at this difficult hour she sensed His strength. Heather had found the one righteous woman she sought. Florinella's prayers for a family for her baby had been answered. As Heather phoned to tell us the incredible news, the Lord spoke: "Change your petitions to praise!" And we did!

The realities of living in a foreign country with an infant became Heather's immediate challenge. Hannah's bed became a little blue plastic bathtub placed between two chairs. Heather's bed continued to be the living room sofa, from which she would pull herself every few hours to feed Hannah. Finally she devised a way to make the nighttime feedings more enjoyable. Hannah would get her bottle, and Heather would treat herself to Germany's chocolate Kinder eggs. She could polish off the egg and put the little puzzle prize together while Hannah happily finished her bottle. Of course the children still practiced their piano and Christi still rehearsed his opera. It was a lesson in patience for everyone!

The legal procedures finally drew to a close three weeks later. Hannah Elizabeth Marie was now an official member of the Beazely family. A baby dedication was planned at the Baptist church to mark the occasion. Everyone involved with Hannah's adoption was invited.

Gabi, Serban, Dr. Stanciulescu, Mariana, Christi, Florinella, and Dorina were all present. So many lives brought together by love and concern for a child. As the pastor pronounced a blessing over the little Romanian baby, a mother's tears fell for the sacrifice made and a young girl's heart basked in the fruit of obedience. God smiled over His children who had stayed the course. Events orchestrated by an unseen hand, revealing the intent of the Father's heart, had culminated in this holy moment. Who would have guessed that this little child would not be the last that Heather would bring home to a new family?

Heather gave Florinella the beautiful silver locket I had sent, along with the Battenberg envelope holding my letter of promise and a Romanian Bible. Our daughter's personal commission from the Father was fast coming to an end—or so we thought.

The pastor repeated a beautiful prayer and blessing over Hannah as the dedication service ended. "'The LORD bless you, and keep you; the LORD make His face shine on you, and be gracious to you;

the LORD lift up His countenance on you, and give you peace.' So they shall invoke My name…and I then will bless them" (Numbers 6:24-27).

Birth mother and adoptive sister stood side by side, invoking the name of the Lord to bless and keep a child who had brought one girl on the journey of a lifetime and another on a journey of the heart. Two young girls, one in need and one looking to meet a need. Two choices, one choosing to give and another choosing to receive. Two cultures colliding. Two countries connecting through unforeseen world events. Promises given, now miraculously fulfilled: "Yet Thou art He who didst bring me forth from the womb; Thou didst make me trust when upon my mother's breasts. Upon Thee I was cast from birth; Thou hast been my God from my mother's womb" (Psalm 22:9-10).

As Moses was lovingly placed in the basket among the bulrushes by his mother, Jochebed, Florinella had lovingly placed her child into the waiting arms of another. Moses' mother and Hannah's mother sought the same thing for the children they loved deeply: the protection and security they were unable to give because of their circumstances. Were these children less loved because of their mother's decisions? No. They were, in fact, loved even more. An incredible sacrifice had been made. Personal desires and longings were set aside to give their children life.

THE HOMECOMING

Ron and I began to prepare Hannah's room. In only a few days, we papered, painted, and hung lace curtains. A beautiful white iron cradle I had purchased came out of the basement and lay waiting for our new baby girl. After so many months, the hope we had grasped by faith was now becoming a reality.

It still seems just like yesterday that we prepared to leave our home to make the drive to the Portland International Airport to pick up our *two* daughters. On the morning of January 13, 1991, nothing could dampen our spirits, not even the break-in that occurred the night before Heather's arrival. Ron actually laughed as he walked inside to tell me someone had broken into the car and pulled out the steering wheel. We simply moved on to "Plan B," borrowing another car and moving confidently forward. "This is going to be a great day!" Ron exclaimed. "The Enemy just had to get one last kick in at the end!"

Birth mother and adoptive sister stood side by side, invoking the name of the Lord to bless and keep a child who had brought one girl on the journey of a lifetime and another on a journey of the heart.

When we arrived at the airport, so many people had come to meet Heather and Hannah that the Delta officials decided to put up a sign on their announcement board telling everyone which gate to go to. The air was full of anticipation and excitement. All three local television stations were on hand to document the day. Even Brie, our dog, got to attend.

Finally the moment arrived. To the sound of flashing cameras and happy screams, Heather walked through Gate 10, cradling our new baby daughter. Both were smothered instantly with hugs and kisses from friends and family.

Ron was the first to take the baby from Heather's arms. Looking at his new daughter for the first time, he began to weep. Then holding her triumphantly high above his head, he proudly shared her with the more than two hundred people who had come to welcome her home. This was a celebration of love, an acknowledgment of faith and courage.

That evening I sat rocking my beautiful baby daughter in her new cradle. There she was, safe and sound in her new room. My heart overflowed with thanksgiving and praise. The words of Luke 1:45-47 came to my mind: "'Blessed is she who believed that there would be a fulfillment of what had been spoken to her by the Lord.' And Mary said, 'My soul exalts the Lord, and my spirit has rejoiced in God my Savior.'"

Our Father has heard the prayers of mothers for thousands of years. The bond between mother and child, whether adopted or birthed, is a miracle performed in the secret depths of a mother's heart, an interchange known and perhaps understood only by the Father. It's a self-sacrificing love akin to His own unconditional love for His children.

On Hannah's first night in our home, I couldn't help but reflect on Florinella's choice to trust our family to raise her beautiful little girl. I knew her arms must ache with the intimate sacrifice she had made. She would carry with her always the memories of that secret birth. I prayed for her wounded heart, that God would soothe her and help her live in peace. I asked God to grace me with what I would need to lead Hannah where Florinella would not be able to go.

I sensed God's presence and His approval as we prepared to parent the new life He had entrusted to us. I remembered the moment so many years ago when I held Ryan on the living room floor. "I am going to give you another child," God had said. As I lay down to sleep on this night with our new daughter in her room across the hall, I whispered a prayer of thanksgiving for a promise fulfilled.

*Ask of Me, and I will surely give the
nations as Thine inheritance,
and the very ends of the earth
as Thy possession.*

PSALM 2:8

CHAPTER TWELVE

A Bigger Plan

Hannah was home. And, at last, so was Heather—or so we thought. Relieved to have our family all together under one roof, Ron and I prepared to settle into a new rhythm of life. Hannah was adapting well, finding her rightful place with her brothers and sisters. However, our plans for a return to normal life were abruptly cut short several days later when Heather announced at dinner that she was going back to Romania.

"I want to do this the rest of my life," she said. "It's my calling. I have to go." She went on to tell us she believed God was calling her to rescue the children of Romania by helping them find families who would adopt them. "God's even given me my first child." My heart flip-flopped, and I whispered a prayer, "Oh Lord, I don't know if I can go through this again. Please help us. This wasn't exactly what I had in mind."

In the middle of my anxious prayer, Heather said, "Mom, remember the woman by the side of the road? Well, she's not a loose end after all."

"A WOMAN BY THE SIDE OF THE ROAD"

With all of the events surrounding Hannah's adoption, Heather had almost forgotten about the woman God had so clearly told her to look for on a particularly discouraging day. That memory and many other painful ones faded into the background the day Heather finally held the child that God had sent her to find.

But several days after Heather found Hannah, Gabi had received a phone call at his apartment. The timid voice on the other end of the phone identified herself as the woman they had stopped to talk with almost two weeks earlier. She was almost ready to deliver her child. Would Gabi pick her up and bring her to Bucharest?

Stunned, Gabi called Heather and told her the incredible news. The woman still expected to give Heather her child. Even though the situation had changed over the past week, they decided to bring the woman to Bucharest. Since Heather was departing for the United States in just a few days, she left some money with Gabi to help care for the woman. Heather promised to return. In fact, she came back to the States with the intention of finding a family to adopt the woman's baby. Of course we didn't know any of this until Heather's announcement.

As Heather shared her heart with us, I was reminded of the words of Hosea—"In Thee the orphan finds mercy" (14:3)—and of David: "Vindicate the weak and fatherless; do justice to the afflicted and destitute. Rescue the weak and needy; deliver them" (Psalm 82:3-4). God was sending Heather back to Romania to administer justice and to extend His mercy to children halfway around the world. His blessing would be Heather's passport and protection.

As my daughter talked, God showed me that Hannah's adoption had not been an end but a beginning. We had not realized what obedience to God's voice would require of each of us. Ron and I had never even considered the thought that something more was up ahead. We had truly only seen one child from one country. God had given us just enough light to keep us moving but thankfully never too much. I think we would have shrunk back in fear if we had anticipated the road stretching before us.

THE BIRTH OF A MINISTRY

Convinced that God had indeed called our daughter to help the children in Romania, Ron and I agreed to help Heather start an adoption ministry. We had no special training for the task at hand. We had only a divine directive to move forward. God did not promise success, but He did promise His presence, and that was enough. In a matter of days we had a name and had filled out the required paperwork to become a nonprofit corporation in Oregon. All God's Children International was born.

The little daughter of the woman by the side of the road was the first child All God's Children International would take out of Romania. God had provided for this child's adoption even before Heather found Hannah. It was a profound lesson for us all, one that we would need to be reminded of many times over.

Once again Heather prepared to leave. Naturally, a million questions and concerns lingered in our hearts. Could Heather bring children out of Romania for adoption? Where would she find the children? How would she cope with the loneliness of living in a foreign land? Would she be able to endure the battles that would come against her soul? These questions and millions more consumed my mind. I knew that we were embarking on yet another journey—a journey that held unknown paths, mountains of victory, and valleys of defeat. But as Heather boarded the plane to Europe just days before her nineteenth birthday, I knew she was in God's hands.

"I DON'T DO NATIONS, LORD"

Six months later I was on a plane, returning home. The jet had just lifted off from Romanian soil, and my heart was filled with grief. The government had announced its decision to close the country to all further adoptions because of the bad press regarding its orphanages. Despite this turn of events, Heather had decided to stay in Romania. She was determined not to give up. In the past six months, she had managed to bring five more Romanian children into new families. With the country closed, what would we do? It seemed like a dead end. As I watched the Romanian countryside below, tears of doubt and fear slid down my cheeks.

Then God spoke to my heart, "I will surely give the nations as Thine inheritance, and the very ends of the earth as Thy possession" (Psalm 2:8). As before, this word came at a time when external circumstances made the promise look as if it could never come to pass. Even after everything our family had been through over the past few years, my initial response was, "Lord, I don't do nations. One country is enough." Yet as the words of Psalm 2:8 settled in my heart, my spirit accepted them as God's promise to our family. I was encouraged and renewed.

Of course I had no idea that in just a few months Heather would travel to Bulgaria to help the children find families. Little did I know then that she would eventually return to Romania and travel to other countries as well to do the same.

THE YOUNG ADVOCATE

The rustic, antiquated elevator that took Heather to the sixteenth floor of the old apartment building in Sofia, Bulgaria, was scarier than any amusement ride she had ever experienced. Frigid temperatures and intermittent hot water and electricity in the apartment would have been enough to send the strongest heart scurrying back to the United States. But this became Heather's home for the next five months, starting in October of 1991.

God had led Heather out of Romania and pointed her toward Bulgaria, a country straining to adopt a democratic government. In fact, until recently her apartment building had housed members of the Bulgarian Communist Party. When she had crossed the Danube River and passed through Rousse on her way to Sofia, she knew that new challenges lay before her. It would not be easy to adjust to yet another country and culture. But the borders inside her heart had already been crossed. The thought of the desperate needs of the children seemed to be all Heather needed to keep her heart focused and her will set.

Soon after she arrived in Sofia, Heather had hired a translator to translate the adoption laws into English so she could familiarize herself with Bulgarian adoption law. She wanted to be prepared for whatever situation she might encounter. Two American families were already waiting for children, and over the next few months God led her to two little girls who needed families. Heather spent the ensuing weeks preparing all the necessary documents.

Now everything was in place, and the long-awaited court date had arrived. All that remained was the arrival of the families, the loving parents who had come so far to meet their waiting children.

THE MOMENT OF JUSTICE

It must have been quite a sight! Two American mothers being led down Sofia's cobblestone streets by our daughter to a waiting car that would take them past the American Embassy to the old brick courthouse.

The two Bulgarian children were too young to realize the importance of this day. They could not comprehend what had transpired over the past few months to bring them to this moment. A new life and a new family would be theirs if only this legal act could be completed. Heather was their lone advocate. She would stand before a

Bulgarian judge and seek justice on behalf of the orphan girls who were waiting even now for their adoptive mothers to come and take them home.

As she led the women up the steps into the building, Heather was struck by its dark, sterile interior. Even the outside natural light seemed to struggle to shine through the old window panes stained gray with age. As they looked for the courtroom, the footsteps of the little group echoed down the old marble hall.

Preparing her heart to stand before the judge, Heather remembered that it was God's job to guard the paths of justice; her job was to follow His lead. She knew that truth and justice were the works of His hands. God was in control. This knowledge calmed her as she walked to the front of the Bulgarian courtroom.

The judge sat high above her on a large, thronelike chair. His long black robe made him look austere and older than he actually was. In reality he was a young man. In Bulgaria one becomes a judge first and then advances to lawyer status. Beside him was a prosecutor. A court reporter sat poised and ready to record every word. The courtroom was quiet. Heather waited for the judge to speak. The two mothers sat nervously behind her.

As Heather leaned forward, she could see the documents that had been prepared over the last weeks laid carefully out before the judge. She watched as he studied them intently. Her eyes watched the hands of an old clock mark off the moments while she prayed she hadn't missed something.

One by one the judge examined the papers—the old birth certificates, the abandonment declarations, the birth mothers' consents, the home studies. The list went on—translations, seals, and stamps. He carefully reviewed them all.

Heather did not know it at the time, but God had sovereignly placed her before a very righteous judge. In years to come this same judge, Mr. Nenov, would become our Bulgarian lawyer. He and his wife, Maria, would work side by side with Heather to help administer justice to hundreds of orphaned children. But at that moment the judge knew that no matter how much he wished to grant Heather's request, if even one point of Bulgarian law had not been satisfied, he would be unable to rescue these little girls from their orphanage life. The requirements of the law could not be changed.

Finally the judge declared that he found everything to his satisfaction. All was in perfect order. Gathering up the documents, the judge looked at Heather and invited her to speak to the court on behalf of the families and children she represented. But first he had a question he wanted her to answer. "Why would an American family who lives halfway across the world travel so far and go through so much to take as their own a child they've only seen in a picture?"

Heather addressed the court, and she did so with holy purpose. Her eyes met the judge's steady gaze. "Your Honor," she said, "these women have come so far because out of all the children in the world, they chose to adopt these children. These little girls were chosen out of love to be part of their families. Your Honor, these children are orphans. They have no inheritance and no family.

"I am here today to help the children, to help them claim their birthright, their God-given right to the love of a family. They are too young to tell you how much they long to be held and rocked to sleep in the arms of a mother. They are too small to tell you how much they wish to spend the day throwing a ball and rolling in tall grass with their fathers. They are too helpless to tell you how they lay in their cribs at night and in their loneliness and insecurity cry themselves to sleep. They are alone, your honor. They have no one to call Mama or Daddy.

"I am hoping you will take to heart the cries of the children, feel their hurt, and understand their plight so that you will closely administer justice and extend mercy to these little ones. The families who sit before you today have met all the requirements set forth by your country. Please rule favorably on their behalf."

We come to God in less-than-perfect condition, scarred and hurt by the action and choices of others. We carry an orphan's broken heart. God chooses us and offers us a place in His royal family.

With those words Heather stepped back and waited for the judge's response. Gazing down at her, he smiled with approval. He was noticeably moved by her words. With a swift bang of his gavel and a quick stroke of his pen, he administered justice that day on behalf of the little girls from Sofia and Pazardjik. Through the strength of God's mercy, these children would soon be safe and secure in the love of a new family.

A few hours later the women traveled to the orphanage to hold their new daughters for the first time. They helped their daughters put on new clothes. They called them by their new names. On that day these two precious children received all the rights and privileges of belonging to a family. Old lives were left behind. These little girls had received their God-given birthrights. They had been sought out, found, and chosen. They were children of promise, lovingly given a future and a hope.

A REFLECTION OF GOD'S HEART

As I have repeatedly witnessed the miracle of adoption, I've come to realize that an earthly judge does not preside alone over these human transactions. From the courts of heaven, another Judge is looking on as well. The earthly process is a reflection of a divine transaction.

Adoption holds a special place in God's heart. After all, He sent His Son so that we could have the opportunity to be adopted into His family. His Son came in mercy and intervened on our behalf when we were helpless. He bought back our empty lives. He redeemed us from the ravages of sin. He gives us His name. Everything He is and has becomes ours. He even gives us a pledge of our inheritance to come.

We come to God in less-than-perfect condition, scarred and hurt by the action and choices of others. We carry an orphan's broken heart. God chooses us and offers us a place in His royal family. The Son goes before His own Father, our righteous Judge, and shows Him the nail prints in His hands and the scars still visible from the soldier's sword.

When the Heavenly Judge asks if the courtrooms of heaven contain all the right documents with all the right seals to guarantee us a place in His family, our Advocate speaks confidently, "Everything is in order. Every letter of the Law has been satisfied. I have paid it all. They were bought with a great price. My blood has covered it all. They stand blameless before you. Their sins, their past lives are gone. This is my child, a part of my family. They are safe in my arms. They are promised a place in my heavenly kingdom. They are joint heirs with me."

Once we understand the great lengths to which God has gone in order to adopt us into His family, we can only exclaim with Paul, "How great is the love the Father has lavished on us, that we should be called children of God!" (1 John 3:1, NIV).

THE BIGGER PICTURE

As I look back on what has unfolded during the past several years, I am awed by what God has accomplished. I've rediscovered—on an almost daily basis—that when we yield in trusting surrender, we are ushered into the very center of His will, further than we dreamed possible.

God's divine direction and the strength of His mercy were first experienced intimately in our home. Our greatest hopes and fondest desires as parents culminated in this amazing journey that our daughter—and our entire family—was called to take. Not only did we hope for the fulfillment of the promise God had given me so many years earlier, but it was also an incredible privilege to watch our oldest daughter walk and talk with the Lord on such intimate terms. To watch her strain to hear His voice and then obediently move forward, even when He didn't explain Himself, was pure delight. It was the most precious gift a parent could ever hope for. Our once-rebellious teenager was transformed into a woman of courage and grace before our very eyes. In the transition, God used her to rescue a needy child—her sister, our new daughter.

Then God invited us as a family to share this same mercy with the world. When I first received God's promise back in October 1985, I could never have dreamed that we would bring more than 300 children out of Eastern Europe to new homes and a new life. Nor could I have imagined that Dr. Vorica Stanciulescu, the doctor who welcomed Heather and led her to Hannah, would eventually gain approval for us to work once again in Romania some four years later. Neither could I have foreseen working in the countries of Bulgaria, China, Russia, Hungary, Macedonia, and Honduras.

In the end all of us were only responding in obedience to what we believe God had called us to do.

> What doth the LORD require of thee, but to do justly, and to love mercy, and to walk humbly with thy God? (Micah 6:8, KJV)

The glory and praise belong to God, and God alone.

> "Not by might nor by power, but by My Spirit," says the LORD. (Zechariah 4:6)

Then I proclaimed a fast...that we might
humble ourselves before our God
to seek from Him a safe journey for us,
our little ones, and all our possessions.

EZRA 8:21

The Journey Continues...

One day almost a year after Hannah's adoption, I received a request for adoption information from a couple in New Zealand. As I prepared the materials for mailing, I remembered that Romona, the little girl we fell in love with in Heather's pictures and set out to adopt, had gone to live in New Zealand. The thought prompted me to include a personal letter, asking if this couple might by chance know through their adoption connections who had adopted Romona. I enclosed an enlarged photograph of her, just in case they recognized the child. I knew it was an almost impossible request. I had no idea where Romona was in New Zealand, but I had to ask.

A few weeks later, I received a phone call. The voice on the other end identified herself as the woman to whom I had written. She thanked me for the adoption information I sent her, and she proceeded to explain that she did indeed know something about Romona.

In that moment, my heart started to race. God's promise to me when we lost Romona flashed across my mind: "I will leave no loose ends in this for you. Just trust Me." Now almost two years later, that promise seemed as real to me in that moment as it had the day I first heard it.

"I can give you some information about her," the woman said.

"That would be wonderful," I responded.

A long pause crept across the phone lines. Then these words fell softly on my heart, an unexpected gift from the Father. "The little girl in the picture," she said, "is my daughter." Tears welled up in my eyes. I realized that out of all the people in the world, out of all the people in New Zealand, this woman had been led to write *to us* for adoption information. She had no idea that we had prayed daily for Romona (now Kiriana) since even before Hannah's adoption!

She went on to say that the picture I sent showed another little child in the background whom they had also adopted, a boy named Christian. Their camera had malfunctioned during their visit to Orphanage Number One, and they had no photographs of either of the children in Romania. She was thrilled to have the picture I sent.

Days later, still marveling at all God had done and the miraculous way He had brought all things full circle, I was able to send this woman copies of all of Heather's pictures from her time at Orphanage Number One. In the box of pictures, I placed the little doll I had purchased long ago in faith for Romona. God had finally tied in this most important loose thread in the fabric of His amazing tapestry. After all, this was the little girl God had used to lead us on our own incredible journey.

Much is written in the Old Testament about the mercy seat, the sacred place in the tabernacle where God dwelled. Each year on the Day of Atonement the High Priest entered the Holy of Holies, seeking mercy for the sins of the people.

Today, because of what Jesus Christ has done for us, we can daily enter into that sacred place. His mercy is available to us moment by moment. The strength of His mercy looked down upon humankind and saw certain death and destruction. The strength of His mercy moved His heart to reach out to adopt us as sons and daughters. The strength of God's mercy took Christ to the cross on our behalf. His strong mercy triumphed over judgment. Through His mercy and sacrifice, He made a way for us to come home.

Just as He has rescued us, we are called to stand in the strength of His unconditional love to embrace the homeless children of the world. He is calling us to redeem lives crushed by the circumstances of their birth. He is calling us to save them, to lift them out. And then, like the Father has carried us, we must carry them in love, with the strength of His mercy...and bring them home.

Although the good-byes don't get easier, and the load
    never lighter,
  the journey must continue.
When days seem long and tiring, and nights restless,
  the journey must continue.
When I see no light at the end of the present tunnel,
    and the future seems frightening,
  the journey must continue.
When my heart is left from place to place, and tears
    mark a well-traveled path,
  the journey must continue.
When my body is weak from travel, and I feel like my
    next step will be my last,
  the journey must continue.
When good memories come to mind, pulling me
    from my present goals and pushing me to
    dwell in the past,
  the journey must continue.
For God has not sent me on this journey to retreat in
    times of trouble or stay planted in a place of
    comfort,
but to press on with a heart set to serve, love to share,
    and strength to continue for His glory!
  The journey must continue.[1]

Key Questions about International Adoption

Adopting a child from another country is a wonderful experience that not only forms a family but usually rescues a child from an orphanage. God commands us to rescue the afflicted, and He promises to make a home for the lonely. Of course adoption is just one of the many ways you can help and rescue those in need.

If you are considering international adoption, I urge you to prayerfully ask the Lord if this is His plan for you and your family. This is not an easy process for anyone, and you'll need the assurance of God's call to make it through the difficult days.

Once you know God's heart on the matter and are convinced He is leading you to international adoption, you can proceed with confidence and joy, knowing that God will guide you on your journey. Remember, He knows all the children by name; you can rely on the strength of His mercy to bring your child home!

To get you started, here are answers to some of the questions we are asked most frequently about the adoption process.

HOW DO I FIND THE RIGHT ADOPTION AGENCY?

There are many Christian adoption agencies here in the United States. It's essential to select an agency that is certified and licensed to work in the country from which you wish to adopt a child. To find a certified agency, you can call the U.S. State Department in Washington, D.C., and receive information on all of the state-certified agencies in the United States, catalogued by the countries in which they work.

Another resource is Adoptive Families of America, which offers a yearly listing of adoption agencies around the country. They also publish an adoptive-parent magazine, *The Adoptive Family Magazine,* and can be reached at 1-800-372-3300.

Choosing an agency usually boils down to your own personal needs and your relationship with those who will help you through the process. Ask for an agency's references; those with happy families will be happy to put you in contact with them.

HOW DO I KNOW I AM ADOPTING
A HEALTHY CHILD?

Your agency should be willing to give you as much information on your child as possible. Videos, pictures, and in-depth medical reports can help a doctor in the United States determine any medical problems or developmental delays that a child may have. Most internationally adopted children suffer from some developmental delay due to lack of stimulation in an institutional environment, so it's important that you get a professional opinion. You will want to be aware of any special needs your child may have.

Find a doctor in your area who specializes in the health issues of internationally adopted children. Your adoption agency should be able to give you a list of physicians who can provide this service.

HOW LONG DOES IT TAKE TO COMPLETE AN INTERNATIONAL ADOPTION?

Generally, it takes between nine months to a year to complete an international adoption. The length of time also depends on how quickly you fill out the paperwork required and how long it takes your agency to complete your home study. Country delays can also happen, so be prepared to wait longer if necessary.

HOW MUCH WILL AN INTERNATIONAL ADOPTION COST?

Costs vary from country to country. Ask your agency about their specific resources and fees. Usually you will be charged an agency fee *and* a separate international fee. You will also need to pay all your own travel, food, and lodging expenses.

The United States is currently offering a five-thousand dollar tax credit to adoptive families. Some employers also provide financial assistance for adoption, so check with your benefits coordinator.

WHO WILL I BE WORKING WITH IN THE FOREIGN COUNTRY?

This is a very important question. Make sure the agency you work with actually owns the country program. This means the staff members you are working with in your child's country of origin answer directly to your agency. Many international adoption programs are operated by individual facilitators who work with multiple agencies in the United States. When this is the case, the agency is often unable to help if something goes wrong when you are in the foreign country. If your agency does not own the adoption program within your child's country of origin, make sure you are comfortable with the in-country facilitator you will be working with.

WHAT DO I NEED TO DO AFTER I BRING MY CHILD HOME?

You'll need to find out about the re-adoption laws in your state. Most states recognize the court decree from the country of origin as final, but in cases where only one parent travels to the foreign country, or if the child has been escorted to the United States by someone else, the state may require the parents to re-adopt.

The U.S. State Department strongly recommends that you re-immunize your child promptly and requires that you naturalize your child as a U.S. citizen as soon as possible. You will also be required to submit periodic updates on your child's progress to your agency. They in turn send these reports to your child's country of origin. The number of updates will depend on your agency and on the requirements of your child's birth country.

HOW DO I KEEP MY CHILD'S CULTURE AND HERITAGE ALIVE?

You can be sure your child's heritage is a rich and exciting part of his or her life by celebrating holidays and other special days that are observed in your child's country of origin. Establish and search out friends for your child from the same country. This can help your child understand that adoption is just another wonderful way that God forms families.

WHAT ABOUT ADOPTION SUPPORT GROUPS?

It is important to get involved in a support group for encouragement once you are home. Adoption support groups can be a source of current information on adoption issues, as well as emotional support from people who understand the unique opportunities and challenges faced by adoptive parents. Most internationally adopted children go through a period of adjustment to their new families, and it is helpful to talk with other parents who have gone through the same experiences.

If you would like more information about adopting internationally, we would love to hear from you. You can call the All God's Children International office in Portland, Oregon, at 1-800-214-6719. Our mailing address is 4114 N.E. Fremont Street, Suite 1, Portland, OR 97212. Or you can reach us by e-mail at agci@usa.net.

Notes

CHAPTER 3: FOR THE LOVE OF FREEDOM

1. Nestor Ratesh, *Romania: The Entangled Revolution* (Westport, Conn.: Praeger Publishers, 1991), 4.
2. Ratesh, *Romania: The Entangled Revolution,* 47.
3. Quote from an interview with an eyewitness.
4. Quote from interview above.
5. Quote from interview above.

CHAPTER 7: WARFARE OF THE SAINTS

1. Ted Mahar, "Schwarzkopf Relates Rules for Leadership," *Portland Oregonian,* 1 October 1993, 4th edition, section C, 5. (emphasis mine)
2. Mahar, "Schwarzkopf Relates Rules for Leadership."

EPILOGUE: THE JOURNEY CONTINUES...

1. Riding on a train just prior to her first trip into Romania, Heather penned these words, which turned out to be almost prophetic.

Bibliography

Bultman, Bud. *Revolution by Candlelight*. Portland, Ore.: Multnomah Publishers, 1991.

"International" column. *New York Times* (December 20, 1989–December 27, 1991).

"Peter Kopvillem." *Maclean's* 103, no. 2 (January 8, 1990): 34.

Nelan, Bruce W. "Slaughter in the Streets." *Time Magazine* 125, no. 1 (January 1, 1990): 34.

Ratesh, Nestor. *Romania: The Entangled Revolution* (Westport, Conn.: Praeger Publishers, 1991).